T0313723

CHSP
HUNGARIAN STUDIES SERIES
NO. 19

EDITORS
Peter Pastor
Ivan Sanders

A Joint Publication with
Gondolat Publishing Co., Budapest

A Possible
and Desirable
Pension System

József Banyár and
József Mészáros

Social Science Monographs, Boulder, Colorado
Center for Hungarian Studies and Publications, Inc.
Wayne, New Jersey
Distributed by Columbia University Press, New York

2009

EAST EUROPEAN MONOGRAPHS
DCCXLII

Originally published as *Egy lehetséges és kívánatos nyugdíjrendszer*
© 2003 by József Banyár and József Mészáros

© 2009 by József Banyár and József Mészáros
© 2009 by the Center for Hungarian Studies
and Publications, Inc.
47 Cecilia Drive, Wayne, New Jersey
07470-4649
E-mail: pastorp@mail. montclair.edu

This book is a joint publication with
Gondolat Publishing Co., Budapest
www.gondolatkiado.hu

Library of Congress Control Number 2008938729
ISBN 978-088033-640-6

Printed in Hungary

A POSSIBLE AND DESIRABLE PENSION SYSTEM
TABLE OF CONTENTS

LIST OF FIGURES AND TABLES

INTRODUCTION

These days, there is much talk in the world of crisis in the large-scale social distribution systems and of the need to reform them. And this goes for the critical situation facing the pension system, too. Street demonstrations targeting pension reform have now become a common sight in major European cities.

Pension systems have a profound and long-lasting influence over the lives of the majority of a population, and they have a major impact on the economic policy and budget of a state. It is therefore of vital importance that caution should be exercised when potential changes are under consideration. The aim of this book is to look at some alternative courses of action.

Our book deals with the issues surrounding the pension systems of developed countries, of societies that are experiencing a second demographic transition, in which the birth rates are falling at the same time as life expectancy is rising.

We will examine in detail the case of a small Central European country – Hungary; partly because we live here, partly because Hungary provides an excellent illustration of the difficulties and the demographic challenges facing the whole of the Central European region as it undertakes economic transformation.

Our book does not seek to become a textbook on pension-related questions. We shall, however, introduce the concepts necessary for an understanding of our argument. These days, social and political questions related to pension systems are the subject of intense academic debate. As with most questions of everyday life, no definitive scientific answer is available.

This book reflects the opinions of the authors, and they bear responsibility for any incidental errors.

***

It is useful to start discussion of the matter by briefly placing the pension system in history, and examining the place and significance of pension in the individual life cycle.

THE DEVELOPMENT OF PENSION SYSTEMS
AND THEIR PLACE
IN THE INDIVIDUAL LIFE CYCLE

The aim of the following brief account is to place the pension systems in history and to ascertain their role in the life of an individual, since the problems of the present-day systems (including the pension system in today's Hungary) and the tasks confronting them should be sought mainly in their genesis and – naturally – their function. The following ideas are – intentionally – in outline form; the aim is not to provide an exhaustive description of the subject matter, but merely to serve as a sort of *basis* for later discussion.

Historico-Logical Background to the Development of Pension Systems

What follows is a kind of thought process, in which we pursue an abstract course of history that does not correspond to the known history of any specific country. We do, however, consider this abstraction to be useful in analysing some important relationships.

History so far has seen the evolutionary path of humanity characterized by people gradually leaving behind their tribal, national and familial ties, and increasingly defining themselves as independent individuals. This process is closely related to the fact that, in the society of which the individual considers himself to be a member, an increasingly multifaceted, refined, comprehensive and structured network of institutions has gradually taken over the integrating and security roles of the tribes, nations, extended families, and other immediate communities. As we go backwards in time, the individual appears increasingly dependent; it is harder and harder to imagine that he could sustain his life away from, or outside of, the community. If he became ill, his family would take care of him. If he became orphaned, an uncle, aunt or a more distant relative would take him in and raise him. If he became unable (or simply too old) to work, once again the family members would take care of him. This solidarity and security, characteristic of immediate communities, gave their members a feeling of security and contentment, since they knew in advance who would take care of them – or vice versa, whom they would take care of if necessary. On the other hand, this kind of arrangement often meant that some members of the community lived under an intolerable burden – one that completely defined the rest of their lives, if they were the ones who had to take care of many others. It must also not be forgotten that the system was closely associated with the relative scarcity of material goods (which we might also call poverty), and this also caused a great fluctuation in the consumption capabilities of some members of the community over time, as their situation depended very heavily on the health, financial situation, etc. of their relatives at any given time. In a world where poverty was the baseline and better years were the exception to this rule, this was seen as the natural way of life.

For these reasons, then, people tried, if at all possible, to escape the burdens that were placed – or that they expected to be placed – on them by society. They did this by increasing the number of people shouldering the burden: the losses and risks faced by the members of the community were spread over an increasingly broad circle, and entitlements became more formalized. In other words, they became institutionalized, and less dependent on the specific individual's burden-bearing ability; and it became less and less expected of individuals that they would bear extreme burdens. This process is also closely linked to the fact that societies became wealthier, and that people's horizons – also closely related – expanded over time. Escaping from the clutches of the necessity to satisfy their daily needs, they had more and more time to plan for tomorrow, and they had more tools available to forestall large decreases in consumption in the future. Experience shows that the *raison d'être* of large communities based on immediate relations is the mutual economic dependence of the people in them, and this is why their members are willing to accept the inconveniences and hardships that stem from living together. As the economic pressure eased, these communities became smaller and smaller, their earlier functions were taken over by social institutions (a much larger, but more impersonal community), and the size of communities based on personal relations approaches the theoretical minimum[1] (father, mother, children), where economic pressure is not necessarily a factor in the decision to live together. (For this reason, we, for our part, consider it flawed logic when certain romantic souls champion family values and inner coherence of large social groups living in poverty. This really is nothing other than economic pressure stemming from poverty, which every nation has passed through at some point in its historical evolution.)

The development of institutions did not, of course, run parallel to the disintegration of the communities, but rather came about through greater or lesser crises (or their development and corrections are still taking place today), and anyway, the break-up of communities[2] has not yet run its course. Often, it only becomes obvious once a community (for example, an extended family) has broken up and that there are no institutions to take over its roles; in such cases, the community is forced to regroup temporarily, and the need to set up an appropriate institution forms into a political demand.

Let us narrow down this general thought process, and apply it to the concrete case of pensions: in the old days, the majority of elderly were cared for within the extended family by their offspring[3] or other relatives. There were practically no elderly people who did not have offspring or relatives. With the break-up of extended families and the loosening of family ties, fewer and fewer elderly people found someone who was able to take care of them, or who felt it to be their duty. With the change in the division of labour, the decline in home (household) production, and the spread of paid work, the elderly could not even help out in the homesteads, as they had previously done.

And so, with the break-up of families and the spread of waged labour, politics found itself faced with a large, unsupported elderly population, whose lack of care gave rise to a feeling of insecurity, both within this group of elders, and within the circle of employed, who came to suppose that they were seeing their own future in the fate of the elderly. Then again, politics was also forced to realize that its exhortations to the active population to save for its old age were largely falling on deaf ears. People somehow always found an opportunity to spend their current income as average income was barely enough to cover current consumption needs, and people always felt that saving and the accumulation of assets was a great sacrifice.

Thus:
- The unsupported elderly caused political tensions.
- Because of this, and for humanitarian considerations as well, these people had to be helped, which placed a large burden on the state budget.
- Most people, unless they were forced to do so, did not accumulate enough assets on their own for old age.

For all these reasons, politics prescribed forced saving for an ever widening set of social classes. The first class was obvious: state employees and workers, who already earned their living from wages, who did not use home (household) production of the family, and where, for these reasons, the old, security-providing families had already broken up. The forced saving was complemented by a system of welfare aid for those people who did not have sufficient income from their modest savings to support themselves in old age. Naturally, this immediately brought with it the free-rider phenomena: "If I can count on social aid in my old age anyway, why should I sacrifice my current consumption to save? I may as well not!" The state – realizing full well that it had to burden the state budget as little as possible by minimizing the amount of aid needed – strictly prescribed and enforced saving.

The situation at this time can be described in another way: the **goal of the pension system** was to force people to plan for their old age, so that they would not need aid, and thus provide them with security and help them avoid poverty.

There are many conclusions that follow from this wording of the goal itself, which will become important later on:

1. It is largely the *relatively* poor, or those without significant wealth in their old age, who must be forced to save, because it is only they that are threatened by poverty in old age (which is why aid is necessary).

2. The mandatory (= roughly "state") pension systems should be general and should encompass most of the population, so long as the population comprises of relatively poor people. As the population becomes wealthier, the pension system can shrink without harming social welfare. In fact, the prescription of forced saving for relatively wealthy people may actually be harmful and dysfunctional.

The system was consolidated, and came to encompass an increasingly wide stratum of society; several generations of workers had the chance to enjoy a pension. Then World War II broke out and all the reserves backing the pension system were destroyed (the factory buildings were bombed, the securities based on them became worthless, the state went bankrupt, and even the government bonds lost their value).

The state, faced with the problem of a large number of unsupported elderly whose lifetime forced savings had been destroyed, handled the situation by taking out a loan and funding the pensions due at the time out of this loan. This borrowing did not involve the usual expedient of printing government securities, but rather the establishment of a new system – the pay-as-you-go system. This system rather concealed the fact that the loan was a loan, and gave rise to all kinds of false speculation regarding the pension system. The mystery surrounding the system was deepened by the fact that the pay-as-you-go system allowed the state to achieve two related, but distinct, goals at one and the same time:

1. forced saving for pension purposes, and
2. income redistribution in old age.

When it saw the apparent success of the system – whose problems were masked by the initially favourable demographic and economic processes – the state gradually extended its scope, so that it continued to borrow, without ever considering the systematic repayment of the loans. The constantly increasing burden of implicit state debt kept getting rolled forward, so that overall, the burden of repaying the loan taken out by one generation was shifted onto other generations.

Problems arose when the demographic processes started to turn less favourable. We could also say that the implicit state debt "bonds" were beginning to expire.

Meanwhile, it should be noted that the (explicitly) funded systems did not, in all cases, go bankrupt, and that not everywhere did the state come to play the main role in the pension system. There remain some funded systems, and there also remain funded and partially funded employer-organized pension systems.[4] This, however, does not change the thrust of the above reasoning.

Nor does it much change the logic that things went in a rather different direction for Hungary and its neighbours after the war. Though the earlier pension reserves were also destroyed in all Central European countries, and the pay-as-you-go system was also introduced, at the same time practically all the tools of production were nationalized. This basically rendered funded pension systems in these countries pointless; or rather, we could say that the pension system – despite its pay-as-you-go nature – was *completely* funded, since there was enormous state wealth backing it. On the principle of implicit state debt, we could even call this phenomenon "implicit funding". During the widespread privatization of the 1990s, however, the implicit pensionwealth nature of the state wealth was virtually forgotten, and in these countries (Hungary too!) a "classical" pay-as-you-go system remained, based on implicit state debt. For us, in this book, this will form the basis of our analysis (though of course we should not forget the other things happening on the pension front in the 1990s). The implicitdebt nature of the pension system is well illustrated by the sporadic suggestions and calculations at the start of the 1990s regarding the use of state wealth to bring about pension reform (Augusztinovics 1993).

Basic Assumptions of Pension Systems

Pension systems, as we have stated, were created to take care of historically homogeneous worker groups in their old age. These groups came from the ranks of the workers in heavy industry or from the group of state employees. At the end of the 19th and the beginning of the 20th century, those working in these occupations were mainly men, and the income and family circumstances of the employees were stable and homogeneous.

Table 1. Development of pension systems

	Industrial accident	Illness	Pension	Unemploy-ment
Australia	1902	1945	1909	1945
Austria	1887	1888	1927	1920
Belgium	1903	1894	1900	1920
Canada	1930	1971	1927	1940
Denmark	1898	1892	1891	1907
Finland	1895	1963	1937	1917
France	1898	1898	1895	1905
Germany	1871	1883	1889	1927
Hungary	1887	1887	1928	1988
Ireland	1897	1911	1908	1911
Italy	1898	1886	1898	1919
Netherlands	1901	1929	1913	1916
New Zealand	1900	1938	1898	1938
Norway	1894	1909	1936	1906
Sweden	1901	1891	1913	1934
Switzerland	1881	1911	1946	1924
United UK	1897	1911	1908	1911
USA	1930	1937	1935	1935

Source: Authors' compilation

Collecting the premiums from the homogeneous worker groups was relatively easy, and avoiding payments was impossible. The society was in a stage of demographic equilibrium or growth, and the economy was in a period of slow but steady growth, so:
- the employment structure was stable
- the demographic situation was favourable, and
- society was in a state of economic growth.

We should point out that the social security pension systems were organized on these three basic assumptions – and continue to this day to rest on them.

As Table 1 shows the 20th century saw the development of state social systems – and was witness to their success story. By the beginning of the 20th century, virtually every developed nation had created a system of social security. In the wake of the Second World War – and depending on the extent of the damage caused by that war – they were, to one degree or another, transformed into pay-as-you-go systems. This process can also be traced through the changes in the structure of the state budget. In this respect, it is especially interesting to compare the United States and continental Europe. The data in Tables 2 and 3 show societies of continental Europe felt the development of a social safety net to be of paramount importance, while in the United States individual responsibility and self-reliance were more pronounced. In the USA, in 1940, the share of direct payments to individuals was 1.4 percent of the GDP[5], lower than anywhere in Europe. The same can be said close to 60 years later in 1998 as shown by table 3.

Table 2. Public expenditure as a percentage of GDP

Country/year	1920	1937	1960	1990
Austria	14.7	15.2	35.7	48.6
France	27.6	29.0	34.6	49.8
Germany	25.0	42.4	32.4	47.1
Italy	22.5	24.5	30.1	53.2
Norway	13.7	19.0	29.9	53.8
Sweden	8.1	10.4	31.0	59.1
Switzerland	4.6	6.1	17.2	33.5
United Kingdom	26.2	30.0	32.2	39.9

Source: Esping-Andersen 1990.

Table 3. Government spending on social programmes as a percentage of GDP, 1998

Country	Total	Elderly, disabled and dependants	Family	Unemploy-ment and labour market programmes	Health	Other
United States	14.6	7.0	0.5	0.7	5.9	0.9
Continental Europe	25.5	12.7	2.3	2.7	6.1	1.7
France	28.8	13.7	2.7	3.1	7.3	2.1
Germany	27.3	12.8	2.7	2.6	7.8	1.5
Sweden	31.0	14.0	3.3	3.9	6.6	3.2
United Kingdom	24.7	14.2	2.2	0.6	5.6	2.0

Source: OECD 1999.

Table 4. The structure of government expenditure as a percentage of GDP, 2000

Country	Total	Consumption		Aid	Social benefits and other transfers	Gross invest-ment
		Goods and services	Wages and payments			
United States	29.9	5.3	9.2	0.1	10.6	3.3
Continental Europe	44.9	8.3	12.4	1.5	17.6	2.5
France	48.7	9.7	13.5	1.3	19.6	3.2
Germany	43.3	10.9	8.1	1.7	20.5	1.8
Sweden	52.2	9.8	16.4	1.5	20.2	2.2
United Kingdom	37.3	11.4	7.5	0.4	15.6	1.1

Source: OECD 2001.

Society functioned within a nation-state framework: it was clear who was subject to the tax and premium payments, and similarly the beneficiaries were also easily defined. International mobility was essentially non-existent, and people more or less lived out their lives where they had been born.

Table 5. Total government expenditure 1982, year of
maximum spending ratio, 2002 (as percentage of GDP)

	1982 or nearest	Maximum public expenditure ratio	Year	2002 or nearest	Change Maximum - 2002
Australia	38.1	40.2	(1985)	35.6	-4.6
Austria	49.0	57.3	(1995)	51.3	-5.9
Belgium	60.8	61.0	(1983)	50.5	-10.5
Canada	46.5	52.8	(1992)	41.4	-11.4
Denmark	57.8	60.7	(1994)	55.8	-4.9
Finland	41.3	60.4	(1993)	50.1	-10.3
France	49.8	55.5	(1996)	53.6	-1.9
Germany	48.1	50.3	(1996)	48.5	-1.8
Greece	35.4	51.0	(1995)	46.8	-4.2
Ireland	49.8	49.8	(1982)	33.5	-16.4
Italy	48.3	57.1	(1993)	48.0	-9.1
Japan	32.9	40.0	(1998)	39.8	-0.2
Luxembourg	49.5	49.5	(1982)	44.3	-5.2
Netherlands	58.6	58.7	(1983)	47.5	-11.2
New Zealand	56.5	56.5	(1985)	41.6	-14.9
Norway	45.6	54.1	(1994)	47.5	-6.6
Portugal	40.0	46.3	(2001)	46.0	-0.3
Spain	35.9	47.6	(1993)	39.9	-7.7
Sweden	64.3	68.0	(1993)	58.3	-9.7
Switzerland	32.8	35.7	(1998)	34.3	-1.4
UK	44.8	45.4	(1984)	41.1	-4.3
United States	36.2	37.2	(1992)	34.1	-3.1
Average	46.5	51.6		45.0	-6.6

Source: EU Commission 1996, AMECO.[6]

Pension and the Individual Life Cycle

In historical terms, even the oldest pension system is a relatively new
development. Basically, it is the product of recent times, and it is
inseparable from the trend that shows a significant increase in life
expectancy at birth. In a sense, the period of "demographic order" has
dawned. One of the most important manifestations of this is the
formation of the standardized life cycle. The standardized life cycle is a
three-stage (inactive, active, inactive) cycle based on economic activity,
and has become widely accepted today, in the sense that every infant
born today has an 80–90% probability of realizing such a life cycle.

Due to the break-up (in the economic sense) of the standardized life cycle and the temporary nature of small community and family relationships, the need arose for some way to regard and treat the financial processes of an individual's life cycle as a comprehensive whole. In theory, this is expressed by the life-cycle models. The main idea of these can be expressed by the following figures.

Figure 1. Break up of standardized life cycle
(relationship between income and consumption)

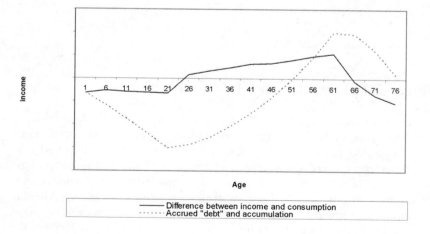

Figure 2. The cash flow of the life cycle

Thus, the average person must earn everything he consumes during his life in his economically active phase (from about 20–25 to about 60–70 years of age). In childhood and adolescence, people only consume, and so they amass a large debt to those who provide for them (for the sake of simplicity, let's call this "society", because childhood consumption is not financed solely by the parents). Childhood consumption (a part of which is education, and socialization in general) can be regarded as a kind of investment by society. This debt is most often repaid, in modern society, when the individuals become adults and raise children themselves – and by their payment of taxes, which are used to finance social transfers. If an individual chooses not to have children, or not "enough" from the point of view of society, then this may be regarded as consumption of capital.

In older ("retired") age, the individual consumes the income he produced during his earlier, active phase, but has not so far used up (at least in the "average" case). Naturally, for this we need some sort of distribution mechanism – a system of institutions that makes this transfer of income possible. In the most general sense, this mechanism, or system of institutions, is what we call a pension system.[7]

A Short History of the Hungarian Pension System

Here in Hungary, compulsory health insurance for workers was introduced by Act XIV of 1881. The first regulation pertaining to pensions applied to those working in the public sector. Act LXV of 1912 created a pension system for public employees, with the system funded directly from the state budget (throughout the world, public sector pensions – where they exist – are usually funded directly from the budget). Act XL of 1928 introduced compulsory retirement, disability and surviving dependants' (widow, orphan) insurance for employees in Hungary. This insurance did not extend to agricultural workers. The the retirement age was 65 years and the mandatory contribution was 5% of gross earnings. After World War II, Hungary switched from a fully-funded system to a pay-as-you-go system that accommodated the prevailing economic and social situation. Act XXX legally binding Decree of 1951 established a complex formula for calculating pensions and set the pension contribution at 4%, paid by the employer. The pension system was made uniform and was extended to virtually every Hungarian citizen by Act II of 1975 (for more on the history of the Hungarian pension system, see S. Szabó 2000). The Hungarian pension system reached maturity around 1970. While Table 6 shows the number of individuals eligible for social security in Hungary between 1950 and 1975; Table 7 shows the number of recipients in the same period.

Table 6. Number of people in Hungary eligible for social security

Year	Own	Dependants' (widow/orphan) right	Together	As a percentage of the population
	Million people			
1950	2.4	2.0	4.4	47
1955	3.2	2.7	5.9	60
1960	4.4	4.1	8.5	85
1965	5.3	4.5	9.8	97
1970	6.2	3.8	10.0	97
1975	6.9	3.6	10.5	100

Source: National Pension Insurance Administration (ONYF).

Table 7. Number of retired, annuitants over time (thousand)

Year	Popula-tion at year's end	Of these, over the age limit*	Number of benefi-ciaries at year's end	Of these			
				retired	accident** agr. co-op*** annuitant	Other**** benefits
1950	9,383		538.9				
1955	9,883		573.7				
1960	10,007	1,718	809.5	613.2		140.3	56.0
1965	10,165	1,941	1,156.0	783.0	34.0	300.0	39.0
1970	10,352	2,131	1,452.6	1,107.4	31.7	279.3	34.0
1975	10,563	2,165	1,801.7	1,500.3	29.4	228.0	44.0

   * Age limit: 60 years for men, 55 for women.
  ** Number of recipients of accident payments before 1964 in number of retired.
 *** Agricultural, collective farm, professional co-op retirement, disability, widow's annuity.
**** Various non-social security transfers, for example: war veterans, blind person's annuity, aid, etc.
Source: National Pension Insurance Administration (ONYF).

In Hungary, the extent of contributions necessary to maintain the system in its mature state, even in the case of the old age pension system, has long been great. (The Hungarian social security system does not treat the different risk factors separately, so the sum of the contributions needed to finance the risks of retirement, disability and surviving dependants are based not on real statistics, but on hypothetical calculations. We should note, that the primary aim of disability systems around the world is to care for those who are permanently forced out of the labour market, and should thus be regarded as much more of an unemployment aid and social transfer than a risk element of pension insurance.)

Table 8. The necessary contribution level[8] by risk (%)

	1997	1998	1999	2000	2001
Old-age	21.5	22.0	22.1	20.8	20.3
Disability	9.0	9.1	9.2	8.7	8.6
Surviving dependant	4.2	4.7	4.7	4.3	4.1

Source: Réti 2002.

Table 9. Disability and accidental disability pension levels at ONYF offices, as ratio of the population in the given county, 2000

County	Ratio	County	Ratio
Baranya	6.22	Komárom	5.89
Bács-Kiskun	5.58	Nógrád	4.46
Békés	8.09	Somogy	4.56
Borsod	5.28	Szabolcs	7.97
Budapest and Pest	3.76	Szolnok	6.19
Csongrád	7.89	Tolna	8.52
Fejér	3.25	Vas	3.33
Győr	3.45	Veszprém	3.86
Hajdú	5.68	Zala	3.04
Heves	6.36		

Source: National Pension Insurance Administration (ONYF).

Table 10. Annual average of registered unemployment rate by county

County	1990	1991	1993	1994	1995	1997	1999	2000
Budapest	0.1	1.2	6.6	5.9	5.7	4.8	3.7	3
Baranya	1.1	5.1	13.2	11.7	11.8	13.3	11.6	11.6
Bács-Kiskun	1.1	5.9	16	13.1	11	10.7	10	10
Békés	1.1	7.4	16.3	15.1	14	13.5	13	13.1
Borsod	2.3	8	20.2	17.5	16.7	19	19.5	20.3
Csongrád	1	4.8	11.7	10.8	9.9	9.2	8.5	8.6
Fejér	1	4.1	12.5	11.3	10.6	9.4	8.3	7.2
Győr	0.5	2.9	8.2	7.7	6.8	6.4	4.8	4.6
Hajdú	0.9	5	16.6	15.3	14.2	15	15.6	14.7
Heves	1.6	6.4	15.2	13.9	12.5	12.1	12.3	12

County	1990	1991	1993	1994	1995	1997	1999	2000
Szolnok	1.6	7	17.1	15.8	14.6	14.8	13.7	13.4
Komárom	1	4.1	14.4	12.6	11.3	11.4	10.1	8.3
Nógrád	2.4	9.8	21.3	17.2	16.3	16.3	16.2	14.9
Pest	0.5	4.4	11	8.1	7.6	7.3	6	5.2
Somogy	1.4	5.2	11.6	10.9	11.2	12.7	12.2	11.9
Szabolcs	2.6	10.7	20.6	19.3	19.3	18.9	18.7	19.5
Tolna	1.6	6.5	14.7	13.4	12.2	13.5	12.9	11.8
Vas	0.4	2.9	9.1	8.3	7.2	6.7	5.6	5.2
Veszprém	0.9	4.9	11.9	10.9	10	9.2	8.2	7.2
Zala	0.8	3.9	10.3	9.8	9.2	9.2	7.7	7.2
National	1	4.1	12.9	11.3	10.6	10.5	9.7	9.3

Source: Labor Office Statistics.

The above tables clearly show that the disability rate is much more closely related to the given area's unemployment rate than to the health status of the area's population. It is surely not conceivable that the people of Vas County (near the Austrian border) are "three times healthier" than those of Békés (in the Southeast corner of the country).

A BRIEF DESCRIPTION OF EXISTING OLD-AGE PENSION SCHEMES

Aspects of Grouping Pension Schemes

There are a number of different types of pension schemes around the world. These are defined on the basis of several basic classifying principles. All systems are based on some basic assumptions and conditions, which will be discussed later on. The most typical dimensions along which the schemes are grouped are and summarized in Table 11:
- the role of the state in providing benefits;
- the role of the private sector in the pension system;
- whether the system is operated on a compulsory or on a voluntary basis;
- the percentage of those in need who belong to the group of insured and/or the percentage of those who are cared for.

Table 11. Financing and provision of benefits in pension schemes

	Community financing	Private financing
Community benefits	Social security	Voluntary participation in the social security system
Private benefits	Compulsory participation, but benefits are operated and provided by companies in the market	Private savings, vocational and workplace pensions

For instance, the Hungarian system of private pension funds is part of the compulsory pension scheme, and it is placed in the second box of the second column. Some pension systems operated by society can have a great influence on the savings pattern and labour market behaviour of members of that society. The status of pension systems as either private or state owned is not directly related to any one particular method of operation; however, compulsory systems are usually – but not necessarily – operated by state authorities.

Table 12. Types of pension schemes

	National	Private
Compulsory	Social security	Compulsory private systems
Voluntary	Voluntary systems	Private savings, life insurances

National pension schemes can be:
- part of the state budget;
- part of the single social security system;
- a separate system.

Compulsory pension schemes usually fulfill different **redistribution tasks.** (In the literature[9] on the subject there is some debate as to whether redistribution forms an integral part of social security pension systems, or whether it should be operated within separate systems. We are going to take a stand on this issue later on.)

Pension systems can be differentiated according to their distributional goals:
- minimal systems, usually providing flat-rate benefits, that seek to prevent poverty in old age, and that are received either on the basis of need or of citizenship (or residence);
- systems proportional to income that seek to enable people to maintain their former lifestyle.

Depending on their construction, systems proportional to income are of two different types: defined contribution (DC) or defined benefit (DB). Both types redistribute income within an individual's life cycle: that is, income derived in the active phase of life is rearranged for the older years.

The relationship between compulsory national pension systems and redistribution is summarized in the following chart:

Table 13. Compulsory national pension systems and redistribution

	Income transfer between individuals	Income transfer within the life cycle
Prevention of old-age poverty	Flat-rate benefit	Based on the payment of minimal pension contributions
Income supplement	Social security with a weak connection between contributions and benefit	Social security with a strong connection between contributions and benefit

The provisions found in the second column of the chart above are mostly characteristics of defined benefit systems, while those in the third column are features of defined contribution systems.

Pension systems can also be categorized in terms of the risk bearer, or the **risk community.** Clearly enough, the extent to which the individual or the community bears the risk determines whether the system is classified as defined contribution or defined benefit. In case of social security, the risk community usually refers to the generations alive at a given time, and it is not possible to divide the risk community into smaller groups with different risks. Thus, it is not possible to calculate different contributions or annuities depending on, for example, gender or family size. There is some debate nowadays, in connection with pension reform, as to whether the whole of society should be considered as one risk community to the end of time, or whether certain generations (or even smaller groups) should be considered as a given risk community. (We are going to take a stand on this issue later on, too.)

The **"pillar"** simile is a widely accepted way of describing pension schemes; it gives a good indication of the mixed systems containing various elements and different kinds of logic. This three pillar system is summarized in Table 14.

Table 14. The usual division of multi-pillar pension systems

Pillar I	• compulsory pay-as-you-go, financed from taxes or contributions, it can be community or private • aim of preventing old-age poverty • pension is proportional to income • redistribution (both between individuals and within the life cycle)
Pillar II	• compulsory or private • funded or pay-as-you-go • state-run or privately operated • defined contribution or defined benefit
Pillar III	• voluntary • funded • privately operated • defined contribution

Generally speaking, the above typology is applied both in literature and in everyday usage. However, it does not provide a perfect description of the complexity of reality. Thus, in countries that have both a flat-rate citizens' pension and compulsory workplace pensions financed through a pay-as-you-go system, either both types are put under Pillar I, or the former is placed under Pillar I, and the latter under Pillar II. In Hungary, for example, by Pillar I we usually mean the "national pension system", which is a compulsory pay-as-you-go system; the system of private pension funds that are compulsory and funded is connected to Pillar II; while voluntary funds and private insurance are referred to as Pillar III. Another possible typology would be if the whole compulsory system – both the pay-as-you-go and the compulsory private-funds system – were put into Pillar I; voluntary funds would belong to Pillar II; and private insurance to Pillar III.

Pension systems[10] are termed compulsory or voluntary, depending on whether or not the state makes it compulsory for its citizens to join the system. **Compulsory systems** are usually **categorized** along three dimensions:

1. fined benefit versus defined contribution;
2. unded versus unfunded systems; and
3. ctuarially correct or fair versus actuarially incorrect systems.

Henceforth, by "defined contribution system" we mean a scheme where the payment rates are the system's external (i.e. exogenous) parameters, while the service provided is the system's internal (i.e. endogenous) parameter. And, vice versa, we are talking about a defined *benefit* system if the system's exogenous parameter is the amount of the later pension, while the pension contribution is the system's internal, endogenous parameter. Defined benefit systems can provide a fixed amount or an amount that depends on previous payments made by the insured.

A system is completely funded if the benefits provided are completely financed by the previous payments and their yields. A system is unfunded if its provisions are financed by the taxes or contributions of the active generation. The latter (unfunded) systems are often called pay-as-you-go systems. In practice, there are several systems that could be placed between these two "typical" systems.

Summarizing the financing and the source of financing of different benefits, we can state the following, as summarized by Table 15:

- A pension scheme can be financed by taxes; in this case, to all intents and purposes, the system forms part of the state budget.
- It can be financed by contributions, and in this case it is separate from the state budget.
- The separate systems can be either funded (explicitly funded) or unfunded (or, as we will see later, implicitly funded).
- Funded systems can be based on the expected value of future benefits, or on accumulated capital.
- In a system based on the expected value of future benefits, the pension paid is the exogenous parameter, and the contribution payable is calculated on the basis of the cover necessary for this benefit, i.e. these systems are defined benefit funded systems.

- In a system based on accumulated capital, contributions are the exogenous parameter, while the benefit received is the endogenous parameter, i.e. these systems are defined contribution funded systems.

Table 15. A comparison of insurance and tax systems

	Insurance system	Tax-transfer structure
Scope of protected people	Selective: only covers certain classes	Universal
Regulation of conditions of entitlement	Abstract, typified	Applying individual judgment
Dominant goal of redistribution	Inter-temporal redistribution of income	Interpersonal judgment
Preliminary condition of remuneration	Yes	No
Basis of financial loading and consideration of entitlement to provision	Similar (or the same)	Different
Dominant approach	Long-term (life cycle) approach	Cross-sectional approach, limited to each period (cross section)

Source: Czúcz 1994.

The actuarial element covers several things. First, in the macro-economic sense, a system is actuarially correct if it is in a state of long-term financial stability. In the microeconomic sense, a system is actuarially correct if the principle of individual equivalence is fulfilled: that is, if an individual's payments into the system and the benefits he receives are actuarially balanced. From now on, we will use the term in the microeconomic sense, as a synonym for "correct".

Table 16. Typology of pension schemes

	Actuarially incorrect	Actuarially correct
Unfunded		
Funded		

Pension systems can be placed in one of the four boxes above as represented by Table 16. Unfunded pay-as-you-go systems can be actuarially correct or incorrect, and, similarly, funded systems may be actuarially correct or incorrect.

Along the first of our trio of typology dimensions, i.e. defined benefit or defined contribution, all four types of systems are possible. For instance, the Notional Nationelly Defined Contribution (NDC)[11] system is a defined contribution, unfunded, actuarially (probably) correct pay-as-you-go system.

This typology is well summarized by the following chart (Table 17).

Table 17. Financing and management in pension insurance

		Formal systems		Informal systems
Main characteristic	National systems	Employment systems	Private savings	Family-based
Compulsory or voluntary	Compulsory	Voluntary or compulsory	Voluntary or compulsory	Regulated by social norms
Redistribution	Yes	Yes	Slight	Within the family
Strength of connection between pension and contributions	Not too strong	Not too strong	Strong	Within the family
Defined benefit or defined contribution	Defined benefit	Mixed	Defined contribution	–
Main risk of the system	Political	Workplace mobility, insolvency of the employer	Investment markets	Common family risk
Pay-as-you-go or funded	Pay-as-you-go	Mixed	Funded	–
National or private management	National	Private	Private	–
Examples	Western European countries	The Netherlands, Switzerland, France	Compulsory: Chile, Singapore Voluntary: UK, USA	–

Workplace pension schemes are quite significant around the world, for instance, 40% of employees in the OECD countries are covered by schemes of this type. As for their financing, there is great diversity: completely funded systems are to be found, as are pay-as-you-go systems.

The Best-Known Pension Schemes

Over the past 150 years, many different kinds of pension system have evolved across the globe. These systems still bear the hallmarks of their birth. According to the simplest typology for the financing of a system, social security pension systems can be pay-as-you-go or funded. A number of countries have systems that are limited to basic old-age benefits – "people's pensions". In some others employer-organized pension funds play a major role; while in others, union-based funds – "mutualities" –are significant. These institutions will shortly be introduced in what follows.

Basic Old-Age Benefit

In a lot of countries where the main element of the pension system depends on individual contributions, the old-age benefit system is used. This does not depend on whether the contribution-proportional system is pay-as-you-go or funded.

Table 18. Basic provisions of social security in EU countries and retirement age for basic provision (cannot be taken earlier)

Basic provision		Basic provision + earnings-related top-up	
Denmark	67	United Kingdom	65
Ireland	67	Luxembourg	65
Netherlands	65		
Finland	65		

* In the United Kingdom, the basic pension instituted by Lord Beveridge could only provide extremely low pensions by the 1970s, so the State Earnings Related Pension Scheme (SERPS) was created to partly top it up.
Source: MISSOC-INFO 2001.

In systems that apply basic old-age benefits, the basic provision is generally a minimum sum close to the minimum subsistence level, and is financed from taxes or tax-related income. In these systems, the retirement age is usually higher than the retirement age of "Pillar II". The retirement age applied in "Pillar II" is usually more flexible than the fixed retirement age for basic benefits. The retirement age for basic benefits is clearly connected to the health and capacity for work of the population in the given society. In most cases, the retirement age is 67 years.

Such systems are operated mostly in northern Europe, where the financing of "Pillar II" is at its most varied. The criteria for entitlement are very diverse. Either residence or nationality is a condition of entitlement, and in some countries the pension received is in proportion to the length of time spent in the country.

The form of provision can be either "means tested", i.e. dependent on income and property inspection, or normative, i.e. given if one meets some general criteria for entitlement. In countries where the system is financed on a normative basis, the provision falls within the tax system and money is clawed back from the higher-income elderly through various tax measures. In our opinion, normative provision is somewhat "more expensive", but is simpler to manage and administer.

The extent of provision and the minimum age of entitlement must be considered. It is worth following the usual practices of other countries, meaning that this minimum age should be higher than the "normal" retirement age.

Old age pension is taxable income in all member states of the European Community, so using the appropriate tax rates the normative basic provision does not need extra resources. To gain a clear picture of the role of the "public pension", let us look at the example of the Dutch pension scheme. In the Netherlands, the public pension system is financed through taxes, and provision depends on a calculation involving the level of the minimum wage and the number of active years spent in the country. Those who have spent at least 44 years in the Netherlands receive a full public pension, while those who have spent less time there get a proportionately smaller amount. Let us look at some simple examples. In the case of someone with an average income, the public pension received will be about 30% of that income (i.e. the "replacement rate" is 30%), while in the case of someone with an income double the average, the replacement rate will be about 15%. Thus, anyone who wishes to get a larger pension in their later years will join the employer's pension scheme (contradictory to next sentence). The employer's pension scheme is included in collective contracts and is compulsory in most companies. Generally speaking, after 40 years of paying contributions, if somebody retires at the age of 65, then this, together with the public pension, will ensure a replacement rate of about 70%. In most cases, employers' pension schemes are defined benefit systems and are index-linked to the rate of increase either in prices or in earnings. Defined contribution pension schemes are becoming more widespread these days, but they are far from being universal.

It is also worth examining the pension scheme in the United Kingdom as it provides a good illustration of the roles of basic pension and supplementary pension schemes. In the UK, males receive a basic pension after the age of 65. Due to the inadequacy of the basic pension, from 1978 the State Earnings Related Pension Scheme

(SERPS) was made compulsory for employees. Employees can, however, choose to contract "out" of SERPS and "into" other pension systems, e.g. workplace pension schemes. Currently, there are about 38,000 defined benefit pension systems in the UK, covering about 9 million employees. There is also a huge number of defined contribution systems, although those cover only about 1 million employees. So we may conclude that, although there are very many funded pension systems, the bulk of the provision actually paid out comes from the pay-as-you-go systems as shown by Table 20.

Table 20. Financing of the UK pension system in 1999

Type of pension	Funded/ pay-as-you-go	Pension expenditure (£bn)
Basic pension	Pay-as-you-go	33.4
SERPS	Pay-as-you-go	4.3
Unfunded public sector pensions	Pay-as-you-go	12.6
Funded schemes	Funded	26.1
Individual schemes	Funded	3.0
Total		79.4

Source: Daykin 2000.

In conclusion, we can state that if a "work pension" is made proportional to payments, i.e. is actuarially correct, then some basic provision must be introduced if old-age poverty is to be avoided. The links between the basic provision, the tax system and "work pensions" are handled in a variety of ways in a number of countries throughout the world, so the task is not simple; but it can be solved.

The Pay-as-You-Go System

A glance through the history of pension systems reveals that, with the exception of the American system, every system was created as a funded system. In the United States, President Franklin Delzuo Roosevelt set up a pay-as-you-go system to handle the problems caused by the Great Depression. That system is based on the simple principle that expenditure and income can be separated within the life cycle of the individual, which means that the pension of the present older generation is covered by the contribution payments made by the present active generation, whose future pensions will be covered by the payments of the active people of the future. Such a system is usually introduced in times when there is an urgent need to tackle old-age poverty – and that usually happens when economic depression or war destroys old people's savings (which could also be in pension funds). Europe had to face this situation after World War II.

Pay-as-you-go systems were thus created on the basis of the previous funded systems, after the accumulations of these systems were destroyed.

A pay-as-you-go system can be either actuarially correct (when the individual's payments and his expected benefits are balanced) or actuarially incorrect (when such a balance cannot be achieved). There are several examples of correct systems, such as the German "earning points" system or the Swedish fund account system (NDC – Notionally Defined Contribution); this latter has served as an example for other countries. The earning-points system and the NDC system are both individual account systems and have very much in common. The main difference is that the earning-points system has a greater degree of flexibility than the NDC: it can set the level of contribution and the level of pension annuity separately, thus enabling the simultaneous existence of a longitudinal and a cross-sectional balance. However, this comes at the price of serious unfairness: there is income transfer between different generations – moreover, the extent of this transfer is invisible.

Devotees of the earning-points system tend to consider this extra degree of freedom to be a clear advantage over NDC. However, with the wage-tax system (which will be discussed later), balance can also be achieved in the NDC; and furthermore, the level of transfer between generations is open and transparent.

If the earning-points system does not utilize the opportunity afforded by that extra degree of freedom, and instead binds contributions strictly to pensions, it loses its ability to create automatic cross-sectional balance. In this case, even if a demographic multiplying factor is introduced, as has happened in Germany, the earning-points system becomes a special form of NDC, where certain parameters are specially adjusted (e.g. wage index for indexation).

Since demographic processes may create extreme situations, it may be impossible to determine contribution and pension annuity independently of one another within the earning-points system. If this happens, the supposed advantage of the earning-points system disappears altogether.

Hungary's pension system is an example of an actuarially incorrect system, where the system contains both open and hidden transfers between different groups of insured.

The German Pension System

In terms of its structure, different parts of the German pension system are clearly separated. The types of benefits provided often differ, as do the methods of determining the amounts of benefit. The basic principles behind its financing and organizational structures are also different. Despite all that, these specific systems can be arranged into three groups. Thus the German pension system as a whole can be described as a *three-pillar system*.

Pillar I, above all, contains the Statutory Pension Scheme. The compulsory system of a fairly large group of wage earners includes workers, employees and some other professions. Besides the social security pension scheme, three further compulsory systems are listed under Pillar I: care of public employees, old age pensions for agricultural workers, and pensions related to certain professions (e.g. the compulsory systems of self-employed professionals belonging to chambers, such as lawyers, physicians, architects, etc.).

Pillar II contains the complementary – and, in Germany, voluntary – company-related old-age insurance and the complementary civil service scheme.

Pillar III means the various forms of voluntary private care, such as life insurance.

There is a minimum level of national care in Germany, provided on the basis of indigence. In the social security system, social aid represents this level. But this does not fall within the trio of the system of care in old age; it functions as an independent system. It aims to ensure the fundamental rights laid down in the constitution, which states that people have the right to such living conditions as enable them to preserve their human dignity.

The pension scheme is managed and operated by its financers, who are divided into groups according to their fields of insurance. They have their own administration, and are separate public bodies. They operate under state supervision, which controls both their financial and their legal operation. Workers and employers are represented on their governing bodies by delegates to the "pension insurance self-government". This consists of a larger legislative and a smaller executive body (though the legislative function is rather limited).

The financers of the pension scheme are:
- Federal Insurance Institute of Employees (BfA);
- Regional Pension Insurance Institutes (LVA);

- Maritime Insurance Fund (*Seekasse*);
- Railway Insurance Institute (*Bahnversicherungsanstalt*); and
- Federal Miners' Insurance Fund (*Bundesknappschaft*).

The German Statutory Pension Scheme is built on the insurance obligation, which means that certain people, as set down in law, must be insured. This affects all employees, the self-employed and certain other groups. But others who fall outside these categories can also choose to be voluntarily insured. Only those groups that have their own systems of care do not belong to the general pension scheme – e.g. civil servants and certain professionals (physicians, architects, pharmacists, etc.). Within the framework of the general pension scheme, all workers and employees – with a few exceptions – are compulsorily insured. People training to be skilled workers also belong in this category.

The German pension scheme is dominated by the pay-as-you-go principle. Contributions paid in today go to current pensioners – a form of solidarity between the generations. The pension insurance scheme holds one month's pension costs in reserve, to make sure pensions are paid. Solvency is thus ensured in case the sector suffers unexpected economic difficulties. Naturally, the state also intervenes if required. Besides the contributions paid by workers and employers, budgetary sources also have a role in the regular financing of the system.

The level of contributions in a given year is determined by a decree issued on 30 September of the previous year. At this point, changes in incomes and in the demographic situation are also considered. No contribution need be paid into the pension insurance on income that exceeds the upper limit of the contribution payment; the insured can choose to make separate agreements for that part of his income. This upper limit can vary. (In 2002, the limit was €54,000 per year for workers and employees in the "old regions" of former West Germany, whereas in the "new regions" of the old East Germany it was €45,000 per year; for miners, the limits were €66,600 and €55,800 per year for the former West and East Germany, respectively.)

According to the principle of mutual and equal burden, contributions defined for a given year are paid by employers and compulsorily insured employees in the ratio 50:50. If the income of a person does not reach the level of the minimum wage, the total amount of contribution required is paid by the employer. Contributions go to the sickness fund, which, as the intake point for social security contributions, forwards them to the pension scheme. (Members of voluntary insurance systems pay their contributions themselves.)

For Statutory Social Security in 2002, the level of contribution in all parts of Germany was 19.1% of gross income, up to the level of the contribution payment limit.

According to the German national rules, the amount of old age pension is determined by the length of time spent in the insurance scheme, by the income earned during this period, by the age of the applicant and by the type of benefit. The amount of old age pension is the product of the following factors:

- earning points;
- correction factor for retirement age;
- adjustment factor for pension type;
- current pension value.

Earning points refer to the income of the individual in every year, in relation to the given year's average national annual income. Earning points are calculated in every year from the average income of the insured population and the income of the insured person in question. If the individual's income in a given year is exactly the same as the average income, he will receive one point; if his income is less or more than average, he will receive proportionately less or more than one point. People collect their points throughout their life cycle. Average gross income for the whole insured population is determined annually, on the basis of data provided by the Federal Statistical Office.

The *correction factor for retirement age*: if the insured reaches retirement age but does not claim the benefits, the size of his pension can be corrected using this correction factor. All extra work means a certain monthly percentage. If the insured retires when he reaches retirement age, the correction factor will be 1.0. (The product of the earning points and the correction factor gives the *personal earning points*.)

Adjustment factor for pension type: this highlights an important difference between various insurance purposes. Old age pension is regarded as the base, and other types of benefit are set in relation to this base.

Current pension value: this is the amount of pension in any given year that corresponds to each point collected. This serves to ensure a balance between fluctuations in earnings and pensions. The amount is determined, with the consent of the Federal Parliament, on 1 July every year, based on the data of the previous year. Pensions are adjusted to the level of earnings by means of the current pension value.

The Employer-Organized Pension Scheme

In most Western European countries employer-organized pension schemes survived. Most of these are funded schemes: the pension fund invests the contribution payments of employers and employees, and the capital accumulated forms the basis of the later annuities. The only exception is France, where the employers' scheme operates on a pay-as-you-go basis. Table 21 below shows the roles of different pension schemes in different countries.

Table 21. Role of the supplementary pension scheme

Country	Employees of the private sector covered %	Funded versus pay-as-you-go	Supplementary scheme as % of the whole pension system, in 1993
Belgium	31	Funded	8
Denmark	80	Funded	18
France	90	Pay-as-you-go	21
Germany	46	Partly funded	11
Greece	5	Partly funded	No data
Ireland	40	Funded	18
Italy	5	Partly funded	2
Luxembourg	30	Partly funded	No data
Netherlands	85	Funded	32
Portugal	15	Funded	No data
Spain	15	Partly funded	3
UK	48	Funded	28

Source: Daykin 2000.

The role of workplace pension schemes is very much affected by the extent of the national pension schemes. Thus, in Europe, the role of supplementary pension schemes is significant in Denmark, Ireland, the Netherlands and the United Kingdom. Besides these, the Swedish system has significant reserves, but in Sweden this is the demographic reserve of the pay-as-you-go system. Table 22 below shows clearly the roles of supplementary and workplace systems in different countries.

Table 22. Capital of the supplementary scheme

Country	Capital, € billion	Capital as % of GDP
Belgium	7	3.4
Denmark	26	20.1
France	41	3.4
Germany	106	5.8
Ireland	18	40.1
Italy	12	1.2
Netherlands	261	88.5
Spain	10	2.2
UK	717	79.4
EU	1,198	20.3

Source: Daykin 2000.

Table 23. Structure of pension systems in European countries and the US

Tier: function	First tier: universal coverage, redistributive				Second tier: mandatory, insurance		
Provision	Public				Public	Private	
Type	Social assistance	Targeted	Basic	Minimum	Type	DB	DC
Austria		yes			DB		
Belgium		yes		yes	DB		
Czech Republic	yes		yes	yes	DB		
Denmark		yes	yes		DB/DC		yes
Finland		yes			DB		
France		yes		yes	DB + points		
Germany	yes				Points		
Greece		yes		yes	DB		
Hungary				yes	DB		yes
Iceland		yes				yes	
Ireland		yes	yes				
Italy	yes				Notional ac		
Luxembourg	yes		yes	yes	DB		
Netherlands	yes		yes			yes	
Norway		yes	yes		Points		
Poland				yes	Notional ac		yes
Portugal		yes		yes	DB		
Slovak Republic				yes	Points		
Spain				yes	DB		

Tier: function	First tier: universal coverage, redistributive				Second tier: mandatory, insurance		
Provision	Public				Public	Private	
Type	Social assis-tance	Tar-geted	Basic	Mini-mum	Type	DB	DC
Sweden		yes			Notional ac	yes	yes
Switzerland		yes		yes	DB	yes	
United Kingdom		yes	yes	yes	DB		
United States		yes			DB		

DB: Defined benefit.
DC: Defined contribution.
notional ac : notionaly defined contribution plans.
Notes on first-tier schemes: "Social assistance" refers to general programmes that also cover older people. "Targeted" covers specific schemes for older people that are means tested. "Basic" schemes are either universal, flat-rate programmes or pay a flat amount per year of coverage. "Minimum" pensions are redistributive parts of earnings-related schemes.
Notes on second-tier schemes: Includes quasi-mandatory schemes with broad coverage. France has two programmes: the public scheme and mandatory occupational plans. Denmark's scheme is a hybrid of DB and DC.
Source: OECD 2005.

A Comparison of Pay-As-You-Go and Funded Systems

As has already been mentioned, with the exception of the US pension system, which was founded during the Great Depression, all pension schemes in the developed world were set up as funded systems. But a significant proportion of these was destroyed in the Second World War and the subsequent economic crisis, so the only way countries could meet the obligations was to turn to the pay-as-you-go system. At that time, the number of beneficiaries was relatively small, so it could have been possible simultaneously to rebuild the funded system and to finance the liabilities of the previous, collapsed system; but in times of post-war reconstruction, governments could not, or did not want to, bear this double burden. Today, however, now that the systems are mature, it would be no easy matter to end the pay-as-you-go system. (A pension system is called "mature" if its accumulation and payout phases are already on a balanced path.) The pay-as-you-go system realizes inter-generational redistribution, since the contributions of those currently active cover the benefits of those who are currently pensioners.

The Level of Contributions

Table 24. Necessary contributions in pay-as-you-go and funded systems, using different economic and demographic assumptions

Interest rate Increase in wages	0.0% 0.0%	0.0% 2.0%	2.0% 3.0%	3.0% 0.0%	3.0% 1.0%	3.0% 3.0%	5.0% 3.0%
Birth rate = -0.5%							
Pay-as-you-go	22.94	22.94	22.94	22.94	22.94	22.94	22.94
Funded	19.77	34.91	26.33	7.70	10.71	19.77	10.84
Birth rate = 0.0%							
Pay-as-you-go	19.77	19.77	19.77	19.77	19.77	19.77	19.77
Funded	19.77	34.91	26.33	7.70	10.71	19.77	10.84
Birth rate = 0.5%							
Pay-as-you-go	16.99	16.99	16.99	16.99	16.99	16.99	16.99
Funded	19.77	34.91	26.33	7.70	10.71	19.77	10.84
Birth rate = 1.0%							
Pay-as-you-go	14.57	14.57	14.57	14.57	14.57	14.57	14.57
Funded	19.77	34.91	26.33	7.70	10.71	19.77	10.84

Source: Thompson 1998.

Table 24 summarizes the necessary contributions in pay-as-you-go and funded systems, using different economic and demographic assumptions. The calculations are based on a simple life cycle: where everyone enters the labour market at the age of 22, works for 43 years, retires on his 65th birthday and lives for 17 years as a pensioner. Pensions mean a replacement rate of 50%, and they increase according to the wage index.

Table 25. The effect of changes in post-retirement mortality on contributions in pay-as-you-go and funded systems

Interest rate Increase in wages	0.0% 0.0%	0.0% 2.0%	2.0% 3.0%	3.0% 0.0%	3.0% 1.0%	3.0% 3.0%	5.0% 3.3%
Remaining life expectancy	Level of contribution						
Pay-as-you-go							
17 years	19.77	19.77	19.77	19.77	19.77	19.77	19.77
20 years	23.26	23.26	23.26	23.26	23.26	23.26	23.26
Funded							
17 years	19.77	34.91	26.33	7.7	10.71	19.77	10.84
20 years	23.26	42.39	31.44	8.7	12.25	23.26	12.41

Source: Thompson 1998.

Table 26. Wage increases, interest rates and the resulting contribution in a hypothetic IS (individual savings) system in four OECD countries

Time period	Germany			Japan			UK			US		
	Wage increase	Interest rate	Contribution	Wage increase	Interest rate	Contribution	Wage increase	Interest rate	Contribution	Wage increase	Interest rate	Contribution
(1953–62)	8.4	3.8	64.2	9.5	5.3	57.7	5.8	1.0	70.5	2.7	1.4	28.6
(1963–72)	6.1	3.9	36.0	7.7	4.3	47.8	5.2	2.5	41.7	1.8	-0.6	39.0
(1973–82)	3.4	3.0	22.4	2.2	2.8	16.6	1.3	-1.2	40.7	-1.2	2.9	5.2
(1983–92)	2.7	5.0	9.8	1.3	3.5	9.9	2.7	4.1	13.1	1.0	5.0	5.7
(1953–73)	7.1	3.8	48.5	8.5	4.6	54.2	5.4	1.7	53.5	2.2	0.3	33.4
(1974–95)	2.6	4.0	12.9	1.8	3.0	14.0	1.8	1.9	19.0	-0.1	4.1	5.1
Total 43-year period (1953–95)	4.8	3.9	25.5	5.5	3.8	28.1	3.6	1.8	32.2	1.0	2.3	13.5

Source: Thompson 1998.

Table 27. Inflation, wage increases, interest rates (data corrected for inflation) in four OECD countries (in %)

Year	Germany				Japan				UK				US			
	Inflation	Wage	Interest	Yield	Inflation	Wage	Interest	Yield	Inflation	Wage	Interest	Yield	Inflation	Wage	Interest	Yield
1953	-2.7	9.6	2.9	21.8	10.7	13.0	-0.8	-5.3	1.6	5.0	-1.9	21.2	-1.4	7.2	1.5	1.7
1954	2.8	1.8	3.1	67.7	1.2	7.7	-0.2	-2.8	3.9	4.8	-2.2	36.5	0.3	0.9	1.0	49.8
1955	1.3	12.3	2.3	21.4	-0.9	18.2	3.6	39.0	5.3	4.5	-1.2	1.9	0.0	5.0	1.2	25.3
1956	1.6	7.8	4.5	-5.5	2.7	3.9	4.2	36.7	3.1	8.7	-0.7	-5.9	3.4	5.4	1.4	4.8
1957	2.1	8.7	5.4	7.7	1.8	6.6	6.4	30.6	4.4	9.8	1.3	-1.4	3.0	-0.5	1.9	-13.1
1958	1.1	7.1	5.8	70.4	0.3	1.0	8.1	-0.3	1.7	8.3	2.1	39.3	1.3	-1.9	1.5	43.0
1959	2.2	7.5	4.2	84.7	1.9	9.4	7.4	35.7	0.0	5.7	4.1	50.3	0.3	4.2	2.2	12.7
1960	0.9	9.9	3.9	34.9	3.7	8.0	7.5	41.6	2.2	3.3	4.7	-2.3	0.0	2.2	1.6	0.9
1961	2.7	9.3	3.0	-8.9	9.3	14.7	8.5	-11.8	4.2	3.6	2.7	-1.6	-0.3	1.0	1.0	27.8
1962	2.9	9.9	2.9	-23.4	4.6	13.6	8.9	-0.5	2.5	4.8	1.3	1.3	0.3	4.0	0.8	-10.2
1963	3.4	4.3	3.5	11.1	6.3	16.1	6.2	-8.0	2.0	8.6	3.6	13.3	-0.3	1.1	0.6	21.8
1964	2.1	4.6	2.7	4.3	4.7	8.4	6.0	0.2	4.9	4.2	2.8	-9.7	0.0	0.8	0.1	16.4
1965	4.0	6.5	3.6	-14.2	6.6	15.3	4.8	16.2	4.6	8.5	1.5	7.3	2.2	0.2	-0.8	11.6
1966	2.9	4.6	4.4	-17.1	4.4	11.1	3.9	6.2	3.5	7.8	2.7	-8.8	3.1	3.1	-0.7	-11.6
1967	0.5	4.2	5.3	49.0	5.7	13.1	5.2	-9.8	2.6	6.1	4.4	35.3	0.3	2.4	-0.7	26.4
1968	2.3	2.8	4.8	13.2	3.8	6.0	5.3	31.8	5.8	3.1	2.4	35.1	2.4	2.6	-0.5	10.1
1969	2.1	8.0	4.8	9.2	6.4	7.9	5.1	34.1	4.7	1.7	3.0	-13.3	4.1	0.3	0.1	-13.4
1970	4.0	13.9	4.8	-26.2	8.1	-15.3	3.7	-20.2	7.9	5.0	2.7	-10.4	3.7	-0.7	0.1	-2.3
1971	5.5	7.5	2.7	3.7	4.8	7.6	2.0	33.3	8.7	2.1	-0.1	35.4	3.3	0.6	-1.7	14.0
1972	6.4	4.7	2.3	8.3	5.9	10.2	1.1	95.1	7.7	5.5	1.9	8.0	4.5	6.1	-2.2	12.9
1973	7.8	5.7	2.2	-21.2	18.2	6.5	0.2	-34.1	10.7	3.5	1.3	-35.5	13.1	0.1	-1.6	-27.9
1974	5.7	7.0	3.2	-4.1	21.0	1.4	2.1	6.1	18.9	2.1	-0.7	-59.2	18.9	-4.5	-0.4	-39.8
1975	5.4	5.2	2.4	22.2	8.0	5.5	3.1	-19.8	25.0	1.9	-7.6	100.6	9.2	-1.5	0.8	26.9
1976	3.7	1.5	3.4	-7.2	10.5	2.8	4.2	9.8	15.1	-1.4	-2.1	-11.2	4.6	1.1	0.7	21.0

1977	3.5	4.7	2.4	6.5	5.0	1.2	3.5	-7.9	12.2	-4.9	-3.0	32.7	6.2	-0.4	0.9	-8.3
1978	-2.5	3.9	3.0	5.3	3.8	2.9	3.3	21.2	8.4	6.2	3.3	0.1	7.7	0.2	2.0	1.5
1979	5.5	2.8	3.2	-11.4	5.7	1.8	3.4	-1.3	17.2	1.4	-1.8	-5.7	12.6	-2.4	3.5	11.5
1980	5.5	2.9	2.9	-2.0	7.2	-2.0	3.6	2.0	15.2	0.9	-5.1	17.4	14.1	-3.9	6.2	17.1
1981	6.8	1.0	3.8	-3.8	4.3	0.3	2.2	12.1	12.0	1.3	0.9	1.5	9.1	-0.2	9.1	-11.8
1982	4.6	-0.1	3.5	9.2	2.1	2.2	2.6	4.0	5.4	2.5	3.1	22.5	2.0	-0.5	8.8	16.3
1983	2.6	0.8	4.4	24.0	1.7	1.3	4.0	26.1	5.3	3.9	5.4	22.5	1.3	1.8	7.1	21.9
1984	2.0	0.8	5.2	6.4	2.7	1.1	4.3	22.0	4.6	0.7	4.9	26.1	2.4	2.3	8.4	0.7
1985	1.7	1.8	4.6	54.2	1.4	1.2	4.1	14.5	5.6	5.0	3.9	14.0	-0.5	0.7	6.8	33.2
1986	-1.0	5.4	6.0	6.7	-0.3	2.2	5.0	49.7	3.8	4.5	5.9	22.7	-2.9	1.4	4.1	19.6
1987	1.0	4.7	5.6	-30.1	0.9	1.9	4.0	10.3	3.7	3.8	4.9	4.0	2.6	2.7	4.6	-0.3
1988	1.8	2.5	4.7	29.8	1.0	2.8	2.9	35.8	6.8	3.2	4.0	4.1	4.0	0.9	5.5	13.4
1989	3.1	1.4	4.2	32.8	2.6	0.9	2.2	21.0	7.7	1.2	1.3	25.8	5.0	-0.8	4.1	23.1
1990	2.7	2.6	6.0	-16.9	3.8	0.6	4.5	-40.9	9.3	0.3	1.3	-17.5	3.7	-0.6	3.6	-9.5
1991	5.3	3.6	5.0	-0.6	2.7	0.1	2.9	-4.1	4.5	2.0	3.9	15.6	0.2	-0.4	2.9	34.0
1992	3.3	3.0	3.8	-9.4	1.2	0.4	1.1	-24.8	2.6	2.3	5.3	15.7	0.6	2.2	2.7	8.3
1993	4.2	1.8	2.1	38.7	1.0	0.7	-0.1	10.3	1.9	2.6	6.0	26.0	1.5	-1.9	2.3	9.7
1994	2.5	-1.4	3.6	-8.2	0.7	1.6	1.1	8.2	2.9	0.3	5.5	-8.5	1.3	0.2	4.1	-1.3
1995	1.8	0.9	4.8	2.9	-0.3	9.4	1.5	1.4	3.2	-0.2	4.7	20.0	3.6	1.1	3.7	31.7

Source: Thompson 1998.

The data above make it clear that the "superiority" of funded systems – that is, a lower contribution needed for the same level of annuity – requires a number of economic and social conditions to be met. For example, with low economic growth and relatively high and steady demographic growth, the necessary contribution level of the pay-as-you-go system can be significantly lower than that of the funded system. We must emphasize that the important factor is *steady demographic growth*, since short-term demographic growth can easily create the illusion among decision makers that contribution levels can be kept lower in the long term. At times of demographic decrease, or when demographic growth ends, there will be a price to pay. It is more favourable to set a "balanced" contribution level and smooth out any fluctuations.

A Comparison of Different Pension Schemes

In the literature of pension systems, there is a huge ongoing debate about the different economic and social effects of possible pension types. This comparison is made along the dimensions of microeconomics, macroeconomics and social policy. Without aiming to be comprehensive, let us mention some of the most popular ideas found in the relevant literature:
  • funded systems are less subject to demographic risks;
  • funded systems have a positive effect on economic growth;
  • funded systems decrease national pension expenditure;

- funded systems have a stimulating effect on the labour market;
- the investment yields of funded systems are usually higher than the rate of increase in real wages;
- private pension schemes reduce undesirable government activity in the pension system;
- state-managed funded schemes are inevitably less effective than private schemes.

These statements are widely accepted in the literature of economics, although they have not been thoroughly proven. In what follows, we present an analysis of the statements.

Statement: There is less demographic risk in the case of funded systems.
Assessment: In a closed economy, the two types of system are similarly sensitive to demographic risks. Let us assume that the system is not closed; then the main question is what possibilities there are for the institutions of the funded system to invest their capital, and what yields they can achieve on the international capital market. It is a widely accepted view in the literature of demography that social security systems – irrespective of their characteristics – reduce the fertility rate (P. Demény has sought to prove this statement in several articles). Every social security pension system results in the children becoming "public property". On the surface of it, funded systems seem to be better protected against ageing, but they definitely discriminate against women who have children, since pensions are determined by calculating the annuity resulting from the capital accumulated. This way of doing things is clearly a counter-incentive to having children. Thus we may conclude that both funded and unfunded systems have a negative effect on fertility, though in different ways.

Statement: Funded systems have a positive effect on economic growth.
Assessment: Despite the fact that this is a generally accepted view in the literature of economics, it has not yet been empirically proven.

Statement: Funded systems decrease national pension expenditure.
Assessment: This statement is true only if the yields that the funded system's institutions achieve are significantly higher than the increase in real wages. Sometimes this is the case; sometimes it is not.

Statement: Funded systems have a stimulating effect on the labour market.

Assessment: The argument behind this statement is that, if the individual's payment is directly linked to his future pension, there is a strong incentive for him to enter and remain in the labour market. In our opinion, this argument is reasonable, but only with the proviso that it should be the difference between actuarially correct and actuarially incorrect systems that are considered here, rather than the difference between funded and unfunded systems.

Statement: The yields of funded systems are usually higher than the increase in real wages.

Assessment: According to relevant data, this is true only for the United States, and has not yet been empirically proven.

Statement: Private pension schemes reduce undesirable government activity in the pension system.

Assessment: It is widely accepted that governments tend to change the rules of pay-as-you-go systems to suit their own interests. Unfortunately, in most cases this is true. (Witness the events of recent years in Hungary.) The argument does not necessarily have to differentiate between private pension systems and state-run systems, since governments have significant influence in every state-run compulsory system. It is essential to make rules that – at least in the medium term – set the pattern of behaviour of the participants and that are respected by everyone. Funded systems may reduce the role of the current government, since all changes need immediate resources to be assigned to them, which means that money is the only information in the system. In our opinion, an actuarially correct, unfunded system also sets limits on irresponsible political decisions. (It needs to be highlighted here that political decisions may be well grounded, but the views of pension professionals may differ from the goals of the political decision makers.)

In our opinion, one of the main advantages of funded systems, or of individual account systems, is that the financial relations within the pension system become clear, i.e. the fact that there is a relationship between individual contribution payments and the pension received later. This is how such systems encourage the insured to enhance their performance. Actuarially incorrect systems are under huge pressure to issue unfunded pension promises. And governments are under huge pressure from pensioners to increase pensions independently of the system, and to change the rules in favour of certain interest groups. (Again, recent years in Hungary serve as a good example.)

Statement: Funded systems managed by the state are inevitably less effective than private schemes.
Assessment: This is not always true; examples can be found both for and against the proposition. It is less a matter of principle than of regulation. (How is effectiveness measured and does this contradict the statement that yields in funded systems are higher than real wage increase?)

On the statements above: in our opinion, important and provable differences between the systems are primarily of a microeconomic nature, causing significant differences in the behaviour of individuals. They thus have a long-term effect. Accordingly, detecting these differences really requires a time-series, rather than a cross-sectional analysis.

The Microeconomic Effect of Pension Systems

Most analyses dealing with pension schemes examine and compare the systems from a macroeconomic perspective. Thus they usually show the invariance of such systems (under certain conditions). In our view, the main difference lies in the *microeconomic* effect of the systems. Let us examine why this is so. Using the typology introduced at the outset, it can easily be seen that defined benefit pay-as-you-go systems encourage people to minimize their own efforts and motivate free-rider behaviour.

The pay-as-you-go systems of numerous countries have many contradictions. The link between the contribution of the individual and the later services is rather loose. The rules have been changed very often in the last decades, what has rendered this loose link more uncertain to the contributors. The situation can well be described by the fact that the contributions of the decisive majority of those who are not paid employee wages are assessed on the basis of minimum wages according to the contribution statistics, that is to say, all that can afford pay the minimal contribution. By our time the pension services have become public goods, hence avoiding or minimising of paying the contribution is a rational strategy to the contributors, if feasible.

In the case of defined contribution pay-as-you-go systems, individual efforts are more directly related to the pensions received later on, which serves as a strong incentive to participate in the pension system.

In the case of funded systems, payments made by the individual and the later receivable pension are clearly connected, so these systems strongly encourage individuals to make efforts within the system.

Pension systems are often categorized according to risk, and it is widely accepted in the literature that pay-as-you-go systems are exposed, above all, to political risks, while funded systems are subject to economic risks. But this is a simplification of the matter. Nowadays we see that both types of system are subject to both kinds of risk. However, different risk factors are realized in different ways within the two kinds of pension system. Let us examine the pay-as-you-go systems first. Pay-as-you-go systems in those countries that are not considered to have individual account defined contribution systems are very strongly exposed to changes in the rules of the pension system. In pay-as-you-go systems, pension promises and actual pensions are separated in time, so legislators often tend to over-promise, sometimes appearing as populist demagogues. In the short term, this seems to benefit most of society, since everyone would like to have higher pensions, allowances, etc. But someone will have to fulfil these promises sometime later on, and even in the medium term this can leave a bitter aftertaste. Another negative effect of such politics is to encourage people's free-rider behaviour. And people also find it unfair if notably different life cycles and contribution payment records result in the same level of benefits.

People then think that their benefits come from an unknown source of the state, so the "state" can increase pensions any time, if resources are available. This gives extra rope to the political demagogue, and means that the current political class could try to gain votes by making (often unrealistic) promises. If so, even the medium-term future of the pension system could be damaged. (It would be worth examining the cyclical tendencies in pension increases and pension promises over the past thirteen years in Hungary.) We may conclude that those pay-as-you-go systems that are not individual account systems are prone to over-promising, because both the people concerned and the political leaders have an interest in overblown promises in the short term. However, such short-term interests can have a very damaging impact on the pension system – partly on account of the unrealistic promises, and partly because they erode consistent cumulative behaviour and promote free-rider attitudes. Because there is a time lapse between a promise and its fulfilment, pay-as-you-go systems generally tend to over-promise, with the political elite buying votes by making unrealistic promises.

Individual account systems, in which individual effort and its rewards are directly related, encourage individual behaviour down the road of consistent accumulation. They also limit the scope for action by politics: resources need to be committed immediately to promises, and these resources are credited to the accounts of individuals. But there is no scope for indulging in politics that favour pensioners, since any measures that do not stem from the logic of the system can only be taken at the risk of damaging the system itself.

Funded systems, on the other hand, encourage the long-term cumulative behaviour of individuals. But these systems, given that they contain very long-term promises – they have to reckon with an accumulation phase of at least forty years – may operate with a large number of preconditions.

Pension Systems in the Countries of the European Community

There is no single pension scheme in the countries of the European Community. The existing systems are based on the member states' traditions, and they reflect the ideas of the World War II period and the restoration that followed. Funded systems play a dominant role in only three countries: Denmark, the Netherlands and the United Kingdom. In the rest of the countries, pay-as-you-go systems predominate, each with a different level of actuarial correctness. Multi-pillar pension systems have been developed in most countries. The pillars are usually defined as below (European conventions in defining the first and the second pillars differ from the convention in Hungary, where the German conceptual system prevails).

- Pillar I: a system providing mostly basic care, financed from taxes, where the criterion for participation is nationality or residence.
- Pillar II: "workplace pension", financed from contributions, where benefits are, to some extent, proportional to contribution payments.
- Pillar III: the system of voluntary, supplementary insurance.

The pension systems of the member states are introduced in the table below.

Table 28. Pension schemes in certain countries of the European Community (Pillar I)

Country	Standard retirement age	Other	Standard retirement age	Other
	Men		Women	
Austria	65		60 (gradually increased to 65)	
Belgium	65		61 in 1998 65 from 2009	
Denmark	67 (basic provision)	At least 37 years of residence in Denmark	67 (basic provision)	At least 37 years of residence in Denmark
Finland	65		65	
France	60		60	
Germany	65		60	
Greece	65		60	
Ireland	65		65	
Italy	65 57/65 with the actuarial correction of the pension in the new system		60 57/65 with the actuarial correction of the pension in the new system	
Luxembourg	65		65	
Netherlands	65			
Portugal	65		65	
Spain	65		65	
Sweden	65 basic pension, 61 "workplace pension"		65 basic pension, 61 "workplace pension"	
United Kingdom	65		Gradually increased to 65	

Source: MISSOC-INFO 2001.

The member states of the European Community use various techniques to make sure pensions follow inflation and changes in economic growth. There are no member states of the community where the pension is not taxable income as stated earlier (page 24).

Table 29. Indexation and taxation in the European Community

Country	Indexation method	Taxation
Austria	Ad hoc, mostly wage index	Normal taxation
Belgium	Price index	Normal taxation
Denmark	Wage index, (if wages rise by more than 2.3%, there is a reduction of 0.3%)	Normal taxation
Finland	Price index for the basic benefit, mixed price-wage index in case of "workplace pension"	Normal taxation
France	Price index with a contingent fix supplement Wage index in the system of civil servants	Normal taxation
Germany	Wage index of the previous year	Special scheme
Greece	Wage index	Normal taxation
Ireland	Price index	Normal taxation
Italy	Price index	Normal taxation
Luxembourg	Price index	Normal taxation
Netherlands	Basic benefit changes according to the minimum wage. In case of "workplace pension" it depends on the fund in question, price index in 15% of the funds, wage index in 65% of them	Normal taxation
Portugal	Wage index in the public sector, while ad hoc in the private sector	Normal taxation with slight modifications
Spain	Price index with a contingent fix supplement	Normal taxation. Special scheme for disability pension
Sweden	Wage index	Normal taxation
United Kingdom	Price index	Normal taxation

Source: Economic Policy Committee 2000.

As we can see, the "official" retirement age is usually between 65 and 67 years of age. The actual age of retirement, however, can diverge significantly from this.

Table 30. Average age of retirement (1998)

Country	Old age	Early retirement	Disability
Austria	64.1	57.9	49.6
Belgium	62.6	55.6	No data
Denmark	67.0	61.0	47.0
Finland	65.4 (64.5)[12]	60.4 (60.4)	49.1 (46.4)
France	61.8	No data	No data
Germany	62.6	—	51.6

Country	Old age	Early retirement	Disability
Greece	60.7	No data	51.4
Ireland	62.0	No data	No data
Italy	61.4	55.6	50.5
Luxembourg	No data	No data	No data
Netherlands	65.0	60.0	No data
Portugal	65.8	No data	53.2
Spain	65.3	60.9	50.3
Sweden	64.5	62.0	50.0
UK	No data	No data	No data

Source: Economic Policy Committee 2000.

The expenditure of social security pension schemes shows significant variation according to the economic and demographic position of the society in question.

Table 31. Expenditure of social security pension schemes as a percentage of GDP (1998)

Country	Expenditure %	Covered
Austria	14.6	100
Belgium	9.5	100
Denmark	10.2	100
Finland	11.5	91
France	12.7	95
Germany	12.4	91
Greece	12.1	No data
Ireland	3.0	100
Italy	14.2	100
Luxembourg	10.6	No data
Netherlands	8.2	100
Portugal	9.8	100
Spain	9.6	97
Sweden	11.5	83
UK	5.3	100

Source: Economic Policy Committee 2000.

A Short Description of the Current Hungarian Pension System

The general compulsory pension system in Hungary dates back to 1 January 1929. Since then, the system has undergone several important changes. The original system took care only of those who earned a wage or a salary. In the beginning, the system was a funded one, but now it is financed mostly through contributions, on a pay-as-you-go basis, and it provides pensions and pension-like benefits. After the 1989 change in the political regime, the first legislation to affect the pension system was passed in 1991. Since then, the pension system has been altered at several different points. The system gained its present form essentially as a result of the "pension reform" of 1997.

Since 1 January 1998, the pension system has three pillars:
- a compulsory pay-as-you-go system, "Pillar I";
- a system of compulsory private pension funds, "Pillar II"; and
- a system of voluntary pension funds, "Pillar III".

The age at which the retirement pension can be claimed is 62 years for both sexes, to be phased in gradually. For men, 62 years is already the normative retirement age. For some hazardous occupations, the retirement age can be lower than this; in that case, though, the insured has to have spent a minimum length of time in the given occupation.

To minimize the impact of the increase in the retirement age, the present pension system makes it possible to retire five years earlier than the normative age, if one possesses a certain number of service years. From 2009 onwards, when the normal retirement age is 62 years for both sexes, it will be possible to retire three years early, if one has at least 37 service years. The retirement age will be influenced by the number of years spent in hazardous occupations; separate regulations will apply in such cases.

As of 2009, to be entitled to a full pension, one must have 20 service years, but even after 15 years a partial pension can be claimed. The pension is calculated by means of a complex formula that takes account of the net income after deduction of contributions and the length of time spent working.

The present pension formula is a highly controversial. First of all, it is not linear in several aspects, and neither income nor service years are treated equally. It is difficult to explain why certain years are considered differently, or why some tranches of contributions paid are treated differently from others. Also, the fact that the system only takes account of whole years can mean the insured suffering significant losses. On the subject of income, the system is even more contradictory, since a "normal" system should encourage people to spend as many years as possible working. This system does not do that: it is not worth having years with an income much below the average, because that can reduce the amount of the pension received.

From 1 January 2013, the pension formula will be radically changed. Those who are members only of Pillar I will receive 1.65% of their average income, multiplied by the number of service years. Members of Pillar II will receive 1.22%, with this amount supplemented by the pension received from Pillar II.

The disability pension system in Hungary does not distinguish between different risks – either in its logic, or in its pension calculation. This means that the old age, disability and surviving dependants' (orphans' and widows') pensions are not separated. This is a source of some contradiction in the relationship between Pillars I and II, as Pillar II – in its present form – is exclusively an old age pension system.

In Hungary, a person is entitled to a disability pension if he has lost at least 67% of his ability to work and, in the available contribution payment period, has racked up the number of service years required by law. The amount of disability pension depends on the degree of disability, the size of the income from which contribution payments were made, and the length of the contributions payment period. The formula used to calculate the disability pension is essentially the same as the formula for old age pension.

The main purpose of a dependant's pension is to ensure that, in the case of the contributor's death, the bereaved should not remain without any support. Widows, widowers and the orphans of active workers with a certain number of service years, of pensioners, and of disability pensioners are all entitled to this allowance.

Widows and widowers are entitled to widow's benefit for one year after the death of their spouse or life partner. Those who are over retirement age, or who receive a disability pension, or who take care of at least two orphan minors, are entitled to a permanent widow's benefit. These rules apply for ten years after the death of the spouse. A temporary one-year widow's benefit amounts to 50% of the full-right benefit, while the permanent widow's pension is 20% of the full benefit.

The orphan's allowance goes to children who are under the age of 16 or in full-time education, up to a maximum age of 25. This allowance is 30% of the full-right benefit, or 60% in the case of orphans who have lost both parents. There is also a minimum set for the orphan's allowance.

Pensions determined and paid in the previous year must be increased in January on the basis of the expected net wage increase and the prices index.

Pillar II has been operating in Hungary since 1 January 1998. The country intends to bring funded elements into the compulsory pension scheme. There are at present still no rules for calculating pensions, but pension calculations become compulsory only after 1 January 2013. Private pension funds (later on in this book simply referred to as "private funds") are, in their present form, the property of their members. (It should be mentioned here that this mode of operation is not customary in the world.) An extensive system of guarantees backs the private pension scheme, so members cannot suffer significant losses, even if the funds do not perform satisfactorily.

According to the present regulations, if a member of the pension fund dies or becomes disabled, he, or his bereaved, can switch back to Pillar I, since Pillar II does not handle any risks from disability or death. (This practice is rather questionable, however, since it is akin to taking out car insurance after having written the car off in an accident.)

Voluntary pension funds have been in operation in Hungary since December 1993. They allow voluntary savings to be collected and to accumulate, in order, to afford the person security in later years.

The system introduced in 1929 was a defined benefit, completely funded system. But that was destroyed by the Second World War and its aftermath. (repetitious) The present pension system is a pay-as-you-go system, financed from contribution payments. Table 32 shows the level of contributions since the 1990s..

Table 32. Gross wage deductions (contributions, taxes and other payslip deductions), 1990–2002

Year	Pension contribution	Medical contribution	Lump sum medical contribution		
	Insured	Employer	Insured	Employer	
	%	%	%	%	HUF/capita/month
1990	10	Together	43		
1991	10	Together	43		
1992	6	24.5	4	19.5	
1993	6	24.5	4	19.5	
1994	6	24.5	4	19.5	
1995	6	24.5	4	19.5	
1996	6	24.5	4	18.0	
1997	6	24.0	4	15.0	1,800
1998	7	24.0	3	15.0	2,100
1999	8	22.0	3	11.0	3,600
2000	8	22.0	3	11.0	3,900

Year	Pension contribution	Medical contribution	Lump sum medical contribution		
	Insured	Employer	Insured	Employer	
	%	%	%	%	HUF/capita/month
2001	8.0	20	3	11	4,200
2002	8.0	18	3	11	4,500
2003	8.5	18	3	11	3,450
2004	8.5	18	4	11	3,450
2005	8.5	18	4	11	3,450
2006	8.5	18	4	11	1,950
2007	8.5	18	4	11	1,950

Source: authors' compilation

CHALLENGES CURRENTLY FACED BY PENSION SYSTEMS

Developed societies have undergone significant change since the 1980s: the demographic balance has disappeared, the structure of employment has changed radically, and thus the financing of a welfare state has become more and more difficult. Institutions operating within the framework of the nation state have had to face up to serious challenges. Economic globalization and transnational institutions above the level of the nation-state have created a completely new situation. These challenges are analysed separately below.

Demographic Challenges

Certain processes that were earlier in evidence have been reinforced over recent decades; thus fewer births and longer life expectancy have meant a shift in the age structure of developed societies. Whereas the elderly used to be in a minority, today the ratio of the elderly to the younger generation has changed dramatically. This raises fresh challenges, since the financing of old-age pensions was originally set up under very different conditions: namely, on the assumption that the active generation would always represent a much larger part of society than the elderly. Given the current situation, decision makers are faced with the prospect of having to raise the retirement age in order to preserve the viability of the pension system in the future. By the 1970s, across the globe, society was virtually totally covered by pension systems. The effect of this is feeding through today.

Table 33. Ratio of the population over 65 receiving benefits in 1939

Country	The ratio of the population over 65 receiving a pension
Australia	54
Austria	35
Belgium	46
Canada	24
Denmark	61

Country	The ratio of the population over 65 receiving a pension
Germany	66
Italy	16
Netherlands	52
Norway	53
Sweden	79
Switzerland	5
United Kingdom	67
USA	5
Average	40

Source: Esping-Andersen 1990.

The data in Table 33 show the gradual maturing of the pension schemes created around the turn of the last century, which, even shortly before the Second World War, covered only 40% of the elderly. Nowadays, pension schemes cover essentially the whole of society.

The pension schemes of European Community states also have huge challenges facing them. According to current expectations, some dramatic demographic changes will occur in the next few decades.

As Table 34 shows increasing rate of the greying of EU.

Table 34. Old-age dependency ratio in the EU

Country	2000	2010	2020	2030
Austria	25.1	28.8	32.4	43.6
Belgium	28.1	29.4	35.6	45.8
Denmark	24.1	27.2	33.7	39.2
Finland	24.5	27.5	38.9	46.9
France	27.2	28.1	35.9	44.0
Germany	26.0	32.9	36.3	46.7
Greece	28.3	31.6	35.8	41.7
Ireland	19.4	19.1	24.5	30.3
Italy	28.8	33.8	39.7	49.2
Luxembourg	23.4	26.2	31.0	39.8
Netherlands	24.9	24.6	33.2	41.5
Portugal	25.1	26.7	30.3	35.0
Spain	27.1	28.9	33.1	41.7
autoSweden	29.6	31.4	37.6	42.7
UK	26.4	26.9	32.0	40.2
EU-15	**26.7**	**29.8**	**35.1**	**43.8**

Source: Economic Policy Committee 2000.

These demographic changes will bring huge challenges for the social security systems of the European Community states over the coming decades. This is especially true of the pension systems, where – in certain countries – dramatic changes in the labour market will cause huge problems in the financing of the existing systems.

Table 35. Total fertility rate

Country	2000	2005	2010	2020	2030
Austria	1.31	1.38	1.41	1.45	1.48
Belgium	1.54	1.61	1.68	1.74	1.77
Denmark	1.77	1.76	1.76	1.79	1.80
Finland	1.73	1.71	1.69	1.70	1.70
France	1.73	1.78	1.79	1.80	1.80
Germany	1.40	1.45	1.47	1.50	1.50
Greece	1.34	1.42	1.45	1.52	1.56
Ireland	1.89	1.85	1.83	1.82	1.81
Italy	1.22	1.31	1.36	1.43	1.48
Luxembourg	1.72	1.74	1.75	1.79	1.80
Netherlands	1.71	1.76	1.79	1.79	1.79
Portugal	1.53	1.60	1.64	1.69	1.70
Spain	1.19	1.28	1.34	1.42	1.48
Sweden	1.50	1.56	1.61	1.70	1.77
UK	1.72	1.73	1.75	1.79	1.80

Source: Economic Policy Committee 2000.

Table 36. Life expectancy at birth (men)

Country	2000	2005	2010	2020	2030
Austria	75.0	75.5	76.1	77.3	78.5
Belgium	75.3	76.6	77.6	79.2	80.1
Denmark	74.2	75.7	76.5	77.4	78.5
Finland	73.9	74.9	75.7	77.4	78.7
France	74.8	75.8	76.8	78.3	79.3
Germany	74.7	75.7	76.6	78.1	79.2
Greece	75.9	76.9	77.7	79.1	80.2
Ireland	74.0	74.9	75.8	77.2	78.2
Italy	75.5	76.5	77.4	79.0	80.1
Luxembourg	74.4	75.8	77.1	78.8	79.7
Netherlands	75.5	76.3	77.0	78.2	79.2
Portugal	72.0	72.9	73.8	75.4	76.8
Spain	74.9	75.4	75.9	77.0	78.0
Sweden	77.3	77.7	78.2	79.1	80.0
UK	75.2	76.1	77.0	78.3	79.3

Source: Economic Policy Committee 2000.

Table 37. Life expectancy at birth (women)

Country	2000	2005	2010	2020	2030
Austria	81.2	81.6	82.1	83.0	84.0
Belgium	81.5	82.4	83.3	84.5	85.1
Denmark	79.0	79.7	80.2	81.1	82.0
Finland	81.1	81.8	82.5	83.6	84.0
France	82.8	83.6	84.2	85.4	86.3
Germany	80.8	81.6	82.3	83.5	84.3
Greece	81.0	81.7	82.4	83.5	84.3
Ireland	79.4	80.2	81.0	82.3	83.2
Italy	82.0	82.7	83.4	84.5	85.3
Luxembourg	80.8	81.7	82.5	83.7	84.5
Netherlands	80.9	81.5	82.0	83.1	84.1
Portugal	79.2	79.9	80.7	82.0	83.1
Spain	82.1	82.8	83.3	84.2	84.7
Sweden	82.0	82.4	82.8	83.5	84.3
UK	80.0	80.9	81.7	83.1	84.1

Source: Economic Policy Committee 2000.

Table 38. Life expectancy over 65, 1996

Country	Life expectancy at age 65	
	Men	Women
Belgium	14.0	18.3
Canada	15.7	19.9
France	15.9	20.3
Germany	14.6	18.3
Italy	15.3	19.1
Japan	16.5	20.9
Netherlands	14.8	19.1
Spain	15.5	19.2
Sweden	16.0	19.8
United Kingdom	14.6	18.3
United States	15.5	19.0

Source: CSO 2001.

Table 39. Ratio of people over 65 compared to people between 15 and 64 (%)

Country	1980	2000	2010	2030	2050
Australia	14.7	18.0	19.8	32.2	37.2
Austria	24.0	21.5	24.0	40.0	53.6
Belgium	21.0	25.2	26.0	42.6	48.3
Canada	13.8	18.7	20.7	37.3	40.1

Country	1980	2000	2010	2030	2050
Denmark	22.3	22.7	25.8	38.4	40.3
Finland	17.7	22.2	25.4	43.5	44.0
France	21.9	24.4	25.3	38.7	44.2
Germany	23.7	24.0	29.6	43.3	48.7
Greece	20.5	26.7	30.3	42.3	64.5
Ireland	18.3	16.8	18.2	28.3	39.9
Italy	20.4	26.9	31.4	49.1	65.7
Luxembourg	20.0	21.2	23.4	37.1	45.2
Netherlands	17.4	20.2	23.0	43.0	49.1
New Zealand	15.7	17.7	18.9	30.4	34.3
Portugal	16.4	23.2	25.2	35.9	56.3
Spain	17.0	24.9	27.0	42.3	72.0
Sweden	25.4	27.1	29.7	43.4	46.5
UK	23.5	24.6	25.9	38.3	42.2
US	16.9	19.0	19.5	33.6	35.5

Source: World Labour Report 2000.

Table 40. Average size of households (number of persons per household)

	1981/1982	1997
EU	2.8	2.5
Belgium	2.7	2.5
Denmark	2.4	2.2
Germany	2.5	2.2
Greece	3.1	2.6
Spain	3.6	3.1
France	2.7	2.4
Ireland	3.6	3.0
Italy	3.0	2.7
Luxembourg	2.8	2.6
Netherlands	2.8	2.3
Austria	2.7	2.5
Portugal	3.3	2.9
Finland	2.6	2.1
Sweden	2.3	2.3
UK	2.7	2.4
Norway	2.7	2.2
Switzerland	2.5	2.3

Source: EUROSTAT 2000.

The social changes of the 1960s, with women starting to work and their educational level increasing becoming higher, and the new values shared by society have resulted in a radical change in the fertility rate over the past thirty years. Whereas in 1960 there was no European country where the fertility rate was below 2.0, today this figure is around 1.5. If these trends continue, then we can expect a dramatic ageing of societies; and even if fertility stabilizes at its present level, societies will have to take care of larger number of old people than now. Unfortunately, the current social systems are not prepared for this. International organizations such as the World Bank, the OECD, and the European Community have embarked on various studies and program- mes to prepare social insurance systems to take care of the increased number of old people. But it is important to note here that, in spite of commonly held beliefs, it is not merely demographic changes that challenge social security systems.

In the 1960s and 1970s, the developed countries met their increased labour demands by promoting immigration. Now these countries have to deal with the problem that integration by the immigrants has been only partially successful. What most countries have done about this problem is to change their immigration policy. But the question is whether economic growth is sustainable with a constantly shrinking labour market. If it is not, then the European Community and the European states will have to reconsider their immigration policies and the issue of integration by immigrants. Such questions will soon arise in Hungary, too.

Several countries have tried to ease the tension in their labour markets by changing their migration policies, but the political events of the past few years have forced these countries to adopt more closed migration policies.

Labour Market Challenges

The classical structure of employment has changed markedly over the past fifteen years. Changes in the structure of the economy have resulted in a decreasing number of people employed in the industrial sector, while a steadily increasing number of people are working in the service sector. This process has changed the classical role of wage workers; atypical forms of employment have appeared; there is a growing number of part-time workers; and the proportion of self-employed has also increased. All this challenges the existing pension schemes, in particular those that are unfunded and actuarially incorrect. The length of time that people are working and paying contributions is gradually getting shorter, while the length of time that they are enjoying a pension is increasing. And they often work only part time during the period when they *are* making contributions, so they are paying less for the benefits of those people already inactive. In those systems that set a minimum provision, part-time employment will often mean that later on people will receive this minimum level of benefit.

Table 41. Ratio of part-time employees in the EU in 1995

Country	Ratio within all employees	Ratio of those who work less than 9 hours per week
Belgium	20.2	0.6
Denmark	24.0	5.2
France	18.0	1.2
Germany	17.4	1.7
Ireland	18.7	1.4
Italy	14.2	0.9
Netherlands	36.7	9.1
Spain	9.9	0.9
Sweden	27.4	2.9
United Kingdom	26.5	4.6

Note: part time is defined as between 1 and 34 hours per week.
Source: Courbier 1999.

Table 42. Ratio of short part-time employment (less than 20 hours) within part-time employment (less than 34 hours)

Country	Men		Women	
	1987	1997	1987	1997
Austria	–	43.9	–	26.0
Belgium	21.5	28.6	34.5	41.7
Denmark	72.6	79.8	39.5	50.6
Finland	–	55.1	–	47.2
France	37.4	33.7	38.9	35.5
Germany	51.6	59.7	32.0	47.5
Greece	21.1	26.5	26.5	27.2
Ireland	30.9	34.7	40.6	41.8
Italy	53.4	57.6	36.3	37.2
Luxembourg	12.9	17.1	38.3	30.4
Netherlands	61.4	70.7	65.9	57.4
Portugal	35.1	41.8	40.1	44.0
Spain	38.6	35.4	47.4	42.5
Sweden	–	48.2	–	30.5
United Kingdom	55.6	63.0	60.2	58.3

Source: OECD 1999; data from EUROSTAT.

Table 43. Ratio of part-time employees according to working hours per week in 1996

Hours per week	Germany				France			
	Industry		Services		Industry		Services	
	Men	Women	Men	Women	Men	Women	Men	Women
1–10	33.9	19.1	30.6	18.4	–	5.1	9.3	9.9
11–20	41.5	47.2	45.3	46.8	37.8	34.9	46.3	36.6
21–24	6.1	8.1	5.9	9.0	(8.0)	10.3	6.3	9.0
25–30	18.5	25.3	18.0	25.4	16.0	20.5	14.0	22.0
31 +	–	–	–	0.4	23.4	21.8	11.6	16.9

Hours per week	Netherlands				United Kingdom			
	Industry		Services		Industry		Services	
	Men	Women	Men	Women	Men	Women	Men	Women
1–10	24.8	28.1	17.7	21.7	26.0	33.2	19.2	22.5
11–20	15.6	26.0	42.3	39.2	34.5	39.1	36.6	41.5
21–24	3.9	7.1	11.9	11.2	12.1	7.9	15.4	12.5
25–30	5.2	11.2	11.0	11.3	18.7	12.5	22.8	17.2
31 +	50.5	27.5	17.1	16.7	7.7	6.2	5.3	5.9

Source: Greiner 1999.

Table 44. Older men in the labour market, employment among 55–64-year-old men (%)

		1960/62	1970/71	1980	1990	2005
Canada	55-59	86.7	84.9	83.9	78.3	75.6
	60-64	75.8	74.1	67.9	54.1	53.2
France	55-59	85.3	82.5	79.8	71.1	62.5
	60-64	71.1	65.7	46.7	22.5	15.4
Germany	55-59	88.7	87.3	82.3	78.6	82.0
	60-64	72.3	69.4	44.2	34.2	40.6
Netherlands	55-59	93.4	86.9	77.2	66.3	77.8
	60-64	80.8	73.9	57.5	22.7	30.9
Sweden	55-59	92.3	88.9	84.4	84.1	85.4
	60-64	76.6	76.6	65.9	63.9	65.1
UK	55-59	99.1	95.2	91.5	81.0	46.3
	60-64		86.5	74.5	54.3	
United States	55-59	88.9	86.8	80.6	78.8	77.6
	60-64	77.1	73.0	60.4	54.1	58.0

Source: ILO.

Table 45. Impact of flexible labour market on the social security system

	Consequences	
	Negative	Other
Structural flexibility		
Unemployment	Restrictive measures for provision of social security Pressure on the care system Demand for a social minimum	Growing significance of unemployment Growing importance of social security Greater social support
Decreasing employment of men	Shorter working phase of life Inactive youth Growing financial difficulties among the old	More time spent in education Early retirement
Increasing employment of women	Growing demand for equal opportunities	Causes partial decrease in employment of men Increasing role of supports for families Presence of the family on the labour market Women receive social security benefits in their own right
Inner flexibility		
Part-time employment	Mostly affects older and younger employees	Common among "second wage earners" Slight changes Low ratio
Forced self-employment Temporary employment	Intensive growth New types of unemployment	Slight changes in the division of jobs
Polarization	Lower classes of society drop out of social security systems	

Source: Greiner 1999.

Relationship Between Pension Schemes and Public Debt

The pay-as-you-go systems have resulted in a significant amount of state debt which accumulated over the past few decades. Such systems aim to create a cross-sectional balance, and so they try to balance income and expenditure within one year. This state debt has two origins: when the pay-as-you-go systems were launched, the contributions to them were set at below the level of "equilibrium contribution", so pension promises and actual payments were not balanced; and higher life expectancy has necessarily resulted in an increase in the equilibrium contribution. This is, in itself, the source of a generational imbalance.

Here we would like to draw attention to a question that is usually not examined adequately. When pension schemes and public debt are analysed, it is important to also examine the portfolios of private pension funds. Pension funds often buy securities and bonds. Later on, these will become the liabilities of later generations, like the implicit debt of pay-as-you-go systems. Because private pension funds are allowed to buy securities, there is often no real difference between pay-as-you-go systems and private pension funds, as expenditure in both cases is covered by the payments of succeeding generations. The only difference is that, in the one case the state debt is implicit, while in the other it is explicit.

Table 46. Accumulated entitlements for pension, as percentage of GDP

(1) Country	Accumulated entitlements as % of 1990 GDP				Accumulated entitlements as % of GDP*	Public debt as % of GDP, 1994 (IMF data)
	(2) Total (3)+(4)-(5)	(3) Current pensioners	(4) Presently employed	(5) Reserves	(6) Total	(7) Total
Belgium	–	–	–	–	75	136
Canada	105	42	71	8	–	96
Denmark	–	–	–	–	87	69
France	216	77	139	–	83	48
Germany	157	55	102	–	138	50
Greece	–	–	–	–	185	114
Ireland	–	–	–	–	55	–
Italy	259	94	165	–	157	129
Japan	145	51	112	18	–	83
Luxembourg	–	–	–	–	156	–
Netherlands	–	–	–	–	103	79
Portugal	–	–	–	–	93	71
Spain	–	–	–	–	93	63
UK	139	58	81	–	68	46
US	89	42	70	23	–	69

Source: Disney 1999. * (Kune 1996, Holzmann 2000).

It is obvious that balancing the budget requires great efforts in certain countries. The level of the possible implicit debt of the systems can hamper (though in a few cases it can prompt) the reforms to be made.

Relationship Between Globalization and Welfare Systems

There are two different aspects of globalization: one is the inter-nationalization of capital and production, i.e. the diminishing role of nation states as economic units; the other is the diminishing legal role of nation states, which is often called trans-nationalization. Both phenomena have a great impact on the pension system. As for the former, internationalization of capital changes many of the conditions of pension schemes, which previously operated within the borders of the nation state. It changes the structure of employment, enhances the mobility of workers and puts pressure on nation states to reduce labour costs, since the labour markets of nation states compete to attract investments from international companies. Global financial companies, on the other hand, try to urge nation states to create funded systems by treating pension reserves as markets. Parallel with this process, globalization goes hand in hand with increased inequality, especially in the less developed countries. In these countries, some people can enter the international labour market and achieve competitive wages, while others have no choice but to remain in the lower strata of a very segmented labour market.

Table 47. Changes in the inequality of income

Country	Wage-income in the mid-1990s			Changes in the division of income		
	lower 30%	middle 40%	upper 30%	lower 30%	middle 40%	upper 30%
Australia	5	34	62	-2.5	-1.9	4.4
Belgium	6	32	62	–	–	–
Canada	9	35	57	-0.5	-0.9	1.4
Denmark	8	38	55	-2.0	-1.2	3.2
Finland	10	35	55	-2.1	-2.3	4.3
France	10	33	57	-0.4	-1.5	1.9
Germany	11	34	55	-0.1	-0.4	0.6
Greece	10	34	56	-1.2	-0.2	1.4
Hungary	7	31	62	-5.2	-1.4	1.8
Ireland	5	31	65	-0.9	-0.7	1.6
Italy	8	31	61	-2.8	-2.3	5.1
Japan	13	35	52	-1.2	-0.8	2.0
Mexico	7	24	69	-0.9	-1.7	2.7
Netherlands	8	36	55	-0.2	0.8	1.2
Norway	8	37	55	-2.8	-1.1	3.9
Sweden	8	35	57	-1.4	-1.5	2.9

Country	Wage-income in the mid-1990s			Changes in the division of income		
	lower 30%	middle 40%	upper 30%	lower 30%	middle 40%	upper 30%
Turkey	8	25	67	-1.0	-3.0	4.0
UK	6	33	61	-0.6	-2.4	3.0
USA	8	33	60	0.1	-1.0	1.0

Source: Förster and Pearson 2000.

The framework of the nation state is challenged not just by the internationalization of production, but also by the internationalization of institutions that formerly operated within the nation-states. This is a process that can also be traced in the development of the European Union.

The institutions of social security have changed radically over the past few decades. Nowadays it is not just international treaties (such as the Universal Declaration of Human Rights or the European Social Charter) that affect them; in the EU especially, the regulation of compulsory pension schemes may (must?) become, at least in part, supranational.

Internationalization of the economy and institutions presents a challenge for nearly every country. Social security systems were set up within the framework of nation states around 1900, but these frameworks are gradually coming to be less able to operate as economic and institutional frameworks. At the start of the 1900s, a nation state, as a single economic area, was a well-defined unit; but the emergence of trans- and multinational companies has forged a new situation. Existing pay-as-you-go systems depend very much on the stability of contribution payers, but increased migration means that a percentage of contributors may well go to another country. This could cause a significant surplus in the target countries, and a deficit in the others. Such processes will be a feature of the coming decades, and, though we have little experience of forecasting them, it is certain that they will present existing social systems with huge challenges.

The challenges outlined above have forced the EU member states to face up to the growing problems. Reforms of pensions systems should be seen both in the context of ensuring adequate and sustainable retirement provision, and in the context of sustainable public finances as a whole and sustainable growth across the EU. The Stockholm European Council outlined a three-pronged strategy to tackle the budgetary implications of ageing populations:

- Member States should reduce public debt levels at a faster pace;
- Member States should undertake comprehensive labour market reforms, including tax and benefit systems, in order ti achieve higher employment rates, in particular among older workers and women;
- Member States should undertake appropriate reforms of pension systems in order to contain pressures on public finances, to place pension systems on a sound financial footing and ensure a fair intergenerational balance.

Six issues are priorities:
- strengthening incentives for working longer;
- developing a life-cycle approach and strengthening the link between contributions and benefits while ensuring adequate income replacement and managing increasing longevity;
- making pension systems more adaptable to structural changes;
- strengthening the role of minimum pensions and of solidarity in pension systems;
- secure private pensions complementing and partially replacing public pension provision;
- strengthening the governance of pension systems.

Challenges Facing the Present Hungarian Pension System

As indeed as is the case throughout the world, the Hungarian pension system has to face up to the challenges presented by an ageing society, a changing labour market, and globalization. Over and above, the general problems that Western European countries have to deal with, Hungary also has to face the losses caused by economic underdevelopment and the changes in the political regime.

Demographic changes have added to Hungary's problems, just as it did for most Western societies. This is partly due to the declining number of births – the fertility rate – and the consequent changes in dependency ratios as shown by Tables 48 and 49.

Table 48. Age composition of the population by age groups, as % of the total population

	0–19	20–59	60–
31 December 1860	46.6	48.3	5.1
31 December 1880	44.5	48.8	6.7
31 December 1890	45.3	47.8	6.9
31 December 1900	44.9	47.6	7.5
31 December 1910	44.7	47.4	8.0
31 December 1920	41.2	49.8	9.0
31 December 1930	37.1	53.1	9.8
1 January 1941	35.5	53.8	10.7
1 January 1949	33.3	55.0	11.7
1 January 1960	33.0	53.3	13.8
1 January 1970	30.0	53.0	17.0
1 January 1980	27.9	55.0	17.1
1 January 1990	27.9	53.2	18.9
1 January 2001	23.1	56.5	20.4

Source: CSO 2001.

Table 49. Age composition, dependency rate, index of ageing

Day, month, year	Age composition %			Dependency rate of children (A/Bx 100)	Dependency rate of elderly (C/Bx 100)	Dependency rate of the population (A+C)/ (Bx100)
	–14 (A)	15–64 (B)	65–X (C)			
31 December 1869	36.7	60.4	2.9	60.8	4.8	65.6
31 December 1880	35.2	61.2	3.6	57.5	5.9	63.4
31 December 1890	36.2	59.6	4.2	60.8	7.0	67.8
31 December 1900	34.9	60.7	4.4	57.5	7.3	64.8
31 December 1910	34.8	60.3	5.0	57.7	8.3	66.0
31 December 1920	30.6	63.8	5.6	48.0	8.7	56.8
31 December 1930	27.5	66.1	6.3	41.7	9.6	51.2
31 January 1941	26.0	67.0	7.0	38.8	10.4	49.2
1 January 1949	24.9	67.6	7.5	36.8	11.1	47.9
1 January 1960	25.4	65.7	8.9	38.7	13.6	52.3
1 January 1970	21.1	67.4	11.5	31.3	17.0	48.3
1 January 1980	21.9	64.6	13.5	33.8	20.9	54.8
1 January 1990	20.5	66.2	13.2	31.0	20.0	51.0
1 January 2001	16.6	68.3	15.1	24.3	22.2	46.5
1 January 2002	16.3	68.4	15.3	23.8	22.3	46.1

Source: CSO 2001.

Contrary to popular beliefs, life expectancy has been gradually growing in Hungary in recent years, especially among people over 60.

Table 50. Life expectancy at birth and at 60 years of age

Year	At birth		At the age of 60	
	Men	Women	Men	Women
1960	65.89	70.10	15.60	17.55
1970	66.31	72.08	15.19	18.19
1980	65.45	72.70	14.58	18.32
1990	65.13	73.71	14.72	19.02
1991	65.02	73.83	14.74	19.15
1992	64.55	73.73	14.52	19.10
1993	64.53	73.81	14.45	19.18
1994	64.84	74.24	14.66	19.32
1995	65.25	74.50	14.77	19.47
1996	66.06	74.70	14.88	19.44
1997	66.35	75.08	14.98	19.69
1998	66.14	75.18	14.95	19.79
1999	66.32	75.13	14.92	19.62
2000	67.11	75.59	15.29	20.04

Source: CSO 2001.

Table 51. Indicators of live births and fertility

Year	Number of live births	Total fertility rate
1949	190,398	2.54
1960	146,461	2.02
1970	151,819	1.97
1980	148,673	1.92
1990	125,679	1.84
2000	97,597	1.33
2001	97,047	1.31

Source: CSO 2001.

It follows from the above data that in the next decades Hungary will have to face up to the challenges presented by the decreasing proportion of young and the increasing proportion of old people (whose number is also growing in absolute terms).

Changes in the Structure of Employment

Before 1990, every person of working age in Hungary was employed. So the social security pension system covered the whole of society in such a way that the insured were paying contributions for a relatively long period of time. After 1990, the structure of employment changed in Hungary, as it did in other central European countries. As a consequence, a large section of people of active age now found themselves excluded from the labour market and from the social security system, both as beneficiaries and as insured. People were also paying contributions sporadically – not like before, when contribution payment was usually continuous. This means that large sections of society will have an incomplete contributions record, which makes it difficult to finance the system at the moment, and to provide for these people in the future. The increasing employment in the "black" and "grey" economies and non-typical forms of employment (e.g. businesses formed out of necessity, minimum wages, etc.) will result in a very low pension for the employees concerned.

Table 52. Economic activity of the population between 15 and 74 years of age

Period of time	Employed	Unem-ployed	Economically active	Ratio of activity	Rate of unemploy-ment
	1000 persons				
1992	4,082.7	444.2	4,526.9	58.6	9.6
1993	3,827.3	518.9	4,346.2	56.0	11.8
1994	3,751.6	451.2	4,202.7	54.0	10.7
1995	3,678.8	418.5	4,095.3	52.4	10.2
1996	3,648.1	400.1	4,048.2	51.8	9.9
1997	3,646.3	348.6	3,995.1	51.2	8.7
1998	3,697.7	313.0	4,010.7	51.7	7.6
1999	3,811.5	284.7	4,096.2	53.1	7.0
2000	3,849.1	282.5	4,111.6	53.5	6.4
2001	3,859.5	232.0	4,092.4	53.3	6.7

Source: Central Statistics Office 2002.

Impact of the Change in the Political Regime on the Pension System

The collapse of the socialist economy resulted in a significant narrowing of employment. At the beginning of the 1990s, some of the unemployed were guided towards the pension system. This resulted in a growing number of people being accepted into the old age pension system, and also in a broadening of the disability system. The latter process was in evidence from as early as 1988. Throughout Europe, the welfare system for the disabled is more akin to a form of constant unemployment than a system of care for the really disabled, and this holds true for Hungary as well. In those regions where the unemployment rate is high, after a short delay the proportion of disabled will also rise; and vice versa, where there is a healthy labour market, there are fewer people receiving benefits from the disability pension system (Table 9).

To sum up, the changes in the political regime resulted in a significant rise in the number of disability beneficiaries, alongside a narrowing of employment. This exerted double the pressure on the social security pension scheme, with fewer people paying contributions and more needing to be cared for.

The 1997 Pension Reform – Problems Resolved and Unsolved

Pillar II of the pension system, in its present form, is in need of significant structural change. Its institutions are now owned by the pension funds' members, but they are controlled by the banks or insurance companies that stand behind them. Let us take a simple example. A private pension fund is established by a financial service provider who invests several billions of forints. Let us suppose that the fund has 150,000 members. The founder institution would like to recover the investment and its yields, but the members are unable to exert real control over the fund. According to the current law, the members bear full responsibility for the operation of the fund, while the institution – which really operates it – has no responsibility. It would be reasonable to transfer the ownership of the private fund and all the responsibility to the founder institution, or to operate it as a new, separate fund; the current set-up combines the disadvantages of both versions, while discarding their advantages. (The negative yields of recent years illustrate this problem quite well – if by yield we mean the projected profit on the total contributions.)

A Possible Answer to the Challenges

Introduction to the Notionally Defined Contribution (NDC) System

Ever since the 1950s, there has been an ongoing debate in the literature about the connection between benefits and contributions. Buchanan published the first article proposing the introduction of "virtual accounts" in 1968. He suggested that pension contributions should be exchanged for pension bonds, which could later serve as a basis for calculating the later pension. He had two versions for calculating the interest on pensions bonds: one was the interest on long-term state bonds, while the other was the current growth rate of GNP. For the calculation of pensions, he suggested the actuarial formula generally used for lifetime annuities.

The NDC (virtual fund account system) was based on this idea. Under this system, contributions paid are credited to individual accounts, where the money attracts interest (different interest rates are possible); then the pension is calculated according to the life expectancy typical of the cohort in question. This idea enables pay-as-you-go systems to operate according to the rules of a funded defined contribution system. Such systems have been totally or partially introduced recently in four countries: Sweden, Italy, Poland, and Latvia. The Swedish version is commonly thought to be the "starting point".

Previously, pay-as-you-go systems operated in all of these countries. Pension outgoings took up 16 percent of the GDP of Italy, 15 percent of Poland, 13 percent of Latvia and 11.4 percent of Sweden. The main incentive to carry out reform was the problem caused by an ageing society.

As was mentioned before, the system is based on the idea that contributions are credited to individual accounts. All countries had to face the difficulty of having to pay existing pensions and, at the same time, of having to set an adequate contribution level for the NDC system. The contribution levels are compared in the following table.:

Table 54. Contributions in Italy, Latvia, Poland, and Sweden

	Italy	Latvia	Poland	Sweden
Contribution	32%(employees) 15% (self-employed)	24%	19.52%	18.5%
Contribution to the pay-as-you-go system	32% (employees) 15% (self-employed)	22%	12.22%	16.0%
Contribution credited to individual accounts	33% (employees) 19% (self-employed)	18%	12.22%	16.0%
Yield	GDP growth	Wage bill index	75% of wage bill index	Wage index
Contribution to the capital-funded pillar	–	2%	7.30% Those born before 1968 can remain in Pillar I	2.5%

Source: Chlon, Fox, and Palmer 2002.

In social security pension systems, it is customary to allow periods when no individual contributions are made (in cases of unemployment, maternity leave, study years, etc.) to qualify as years towards entitlement. This is also possible in an NDC system, but the underlying financial processes must be made explicit – i.e. only contributions can result in entitlement. This is the case in the four countries mentioned above: they do allow different periods of time to qualify as years towards entitlement, and the amounts differ from country to country, but in all cases the state has to pay contributions to the individual accounts.

Provisions

The life expectancy of the cohort in question is taken into account when the pensions are calculated in the NDC systems of all the countries. In Italy and Sweden, the figures for life expectancy are modified for economic growth. In all the countries, pensions are indexed using one method or another.

Table 55. Divisor of pension formula and indexation of pensions

	Italy	Latvia	Poland	Sweden
Modification of the divisor of the pension formula	Life expectancy corrected by 1.5% expected GDP growth	No	No	Corrected by 1.6% rate of return
Indexation of pension	Price index	Wage index	Mixed price-wage index	Price index with slight modification

Source: Chlon, Fox, and Palmer 2002.

The formula is: $P_n = \dfrac{\sum_{j=k}^{n} \left(cw_j \prod_{j=i}^{n} (1 + I_j) \right)}{G_{n,r,s}}$

P_n: the sum of contributions in year n
c: the contribution level
w_j: the contribution base in year j
I_j: the indexation of the capital in year j
k: the age when contribution was first paid
G: annuity

Where:
c – contribution level
The size of the pension depends directly on the contributions paid in, so the contribution level must be enough to ensure that the pension is higher than the poverty threshold. The formula shows clearly the relationship between the contribution level and the pension.

I_j – index rate of the accumulation period
Indexation of the accounts is one of the most important components in the long-term stability of the system. There are several solutions for indexation (inflation, average growth in earnings, GDP growth, yields of state bonds), but there is no consensus yet in the literature on the subject of its correct level.

w_j – contribution base
The basis for the payment of contributions is usually the wage of the insured, but it may be something different, depending on the government's insurance policy; there may be a cap on the income on which contributions are paid, and the government may pay support for periods when the insured has no wages (military service, maternity leave, etc.).

G – annuity

Its usual level in literature is the unisex life expectancy in the year of retirement. (This means that the risk community is considered to be people born in a given year.) When the annuity is determined, benefits for widow/ers and orphans are usually set and indexation of the pension is also determined.

A major function of social security pension systems is to cut out poverty in old age, so most schemes guarantee some kind of minimal pension. This is also true of the NDC systems. Since the provisions of this system depend on the contributions paid in, there are many people who – for various reasons – have been unable to pay in enough to receive a satisfactory pension. Other, complementary, provisions are made for such people – a process often called pillar "zero". Such payments are either normative or means tested. The four countries above tackle this issue in different ways, but in each case the state allocates some of its income from other sources to pillar zero, in order to maintain it. Let us consider the Swedish example. In Sweden, a minimum old age provision exists alongside the NDC system. This safeguards the minimum pension. This minimum old-age provision can be received in addition to any pension coming in from the NDC, if the recipient is at the lower end of the pension scale. Calculation of this pension is rather complicated, but is well illustrated in the following diagram.

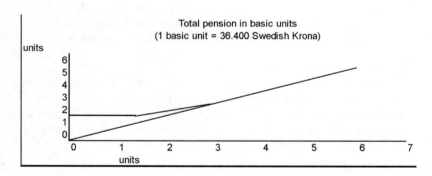

Figure 3. Basic pension in Sweden
(a unit is SKR 36,400/2001)

A fundamental feature of the minimum provision is that it can only be received over a certain age, whereas the NDC system permits a more flexible retirement age. For instance, the minimum provision in

Sweden can only be received over the age of 65, but the NDC system allows retirement at age 60.

Other Features of the NDC System

Since cohorts are regarded as the risk communities, if an insured dies during his active period, in most systems his accumulated contributions are "inherited" by his cohort. This is not the case in funded systems, where the amount accumulated is inherited by the heirs of the insured.

Most systems possess a demographic reserve; moreover, funded pillars have been established to complement all of them. (One great advantage of the NDC system is that, if the state budget is in surplus, the ratio between the pay-as-you-go and the funded systems can be altered.) When NDC systems were first introduced, an important point was whether and how to incorporate disability pensions and dependants' allowances into the new system. The four countries chose different ways of tackling this issue.

Reserve

The longitudinal balance of the system does not automatically create a cross-sectional balance. Economic fluctuations may also have an effect on the balance of contributions received and pensions paid. This is why reserves are essential. (It should be mentioned that, if a pension fund is autonomous and managed responsibly, most countries have reserve funds. Thus, it is not just NDC systems that have reserve funds.) In Sweden, a demographic reserve was created back in 1960, when the general "complementary" system was launched. The amount of this reserve now equals 41 percent of the country's GDP.

Transition from the Old System to the New

The transition in all the countries was achieved with two points kept firmly in mind: first, generations close to retirement should not be affected by the new system, and second, the system had to remain capable of being financed. The rules governing transition are summarized in the following chart:

Table 56. Rules of transition to the NDC system

	Italy	Latvia	Poland	Sweden
Countries concerned in the NDC				
Coverage	In cases where there are fewer than 18 service years, the new system is compulsory; where there are more than 18 service years it is voluntary. Those who gained entitlement before 1995 receive a pension calculated in a mixed way	Everybody	Compulsory under 50	Mixed pension during the period of transition
The oldest generation in the NDC	Compulsory: 1960 Optional: 1936	1936	1949	1938
First generation to whom NDC fully applies	1978	1981	1981	1953
Joining of the funded system				
Optional or otherwise		Compulsory under the age of 30, optional between 30 and 49 years of age	Compulsory under the age of 30, optional between 30 and 50 years of age	Compulsory
Oldest generation concerned		1951	1949	

Source: Chlon, Fox, and Palmer 2002.

It can easily be seen that there are considerable differences between the countries, but a transitional period was set in each of them.

Rules of Transition

The main difficulty during transition is the question of how former entitlements should be acknowledged in the new system. This is particularly difficult in those countries where no adequate data are available about contributions made by the insured. (This also applies to Hungary, as full income data have only been available since 1988.) In several countries, pension was calculated according to the former rules, and then it was capitalized. The exact methods vary from country to country. In Italy, pensions have been calculated according to the rules of the NDC system since 1996, while entitlements dating from before

1996 are calculated according to the former rules. Transition thus becomes relatively easy, though it does take a long time. In Sweden, the pensions of people born between 1938 and 1953 are calculated according to both systems, and the results are weighted using different methods. For those people born in 1938, 80 percent of their pension is calculated according to the old system, while 20 percent is calculated according to the new rules. People born in 1954 have their pensions calculated according to the new system. (The Swedish system has a precise record of the past.)

In Latvia and in Poland, starting capital is calculated by applying various, rather complicated, rules. Neither of these countries has precise data about their past.

In all four countries, transition to the NDC system – with its concomitant actuarial approach – has promoted long-term macro stability. Though this macro stability may well be good for the national economy in general, it must be said that the resulting decline in pensions has been rather a bitter pill to swallow for the individuals concerned.

CONCEPTUAL PROBLEMS RELATED TO PENSION SYSTEMS

In this chapter we would like to examine a few concepts and principles that are unavoidable in any discussion of pension systems and their reform. Let us start with the function of a pension system.

What is a Pension System for?

A pension system is one of the large social security systems, and its function can only to some extent be separated from the function ing of other elements of these security systems (primarily the widows' orphans' and disability benefits and the health insurance systems).

The development of the present form of today's large-scale social security systems is related to the large-scale transformation of society and the crisis connected to this transformation. The essence of this transformation is the development of the nation state and, in parallel with this, the development of a unified national economy. As the social projection of this process, the traditional family, kinship, village and professional communities have vanished along with the traditional relationships; in the absence of these old communities, the security systems have had to be reorganized on a new, large, community level – at the "national" level (which is why we can call these systems "large-scale"). This national aspect of the systems is a built-in feature, and most of the time is taken for granted and causes no problems; however, at the same time it brings with it boundaries and limitations that will make themselves felt in the (not too distant) future.

The subject of these large social security systems is the whole population – or the whole affected population. At first (and indeed for a long time after) individual equivalence is not considered – the concept does not exist, so it cannot arise as a problem. The history of these systems – including the history of the pension system – can be viewed as the history of the expansion of the affected population. In this respect, the process has today peaked: it is physically impossible to draw any more classes into the system within the national state (at least in the developed industrial countries).

The pension system often appears as the state caring and providing for its citizens. And this is often the way matters are presented. In reality, however, it is more appropriate to regard it rather as the state "thinking" of its people in advance, and employing compulsory measures to make the large mass of the population look to the future. This way the pension system can also be regarded as a compulsory saving mechanism, whose goal it is to prevent large swathes of the population from suffering a drastic fall in their standard of living in old age – and possibly penury.

Pension systems have been evolving along several parallel lines, and the evolution of these parallel lines continues to the present day. The development of private insurance based on individual equivalence (mainly through annuity insurance provided for the better off) began right at the outset, along with the formation of pension funds, the provision of additional benefits for certain employees in some enterprises, and the payment of the state pension to state employees (e.g. teachers, military officers). Of these, the state-organized pension system is today the most widespread and the most general. In the various systems, the principle of individual equivalence is met to differing extents: it is best fulfilled in private insurance, and least in the state system.

The state-organized pension system very often copies traditional solutions to security, i.e. the participants in these systems can often be regarded as a "solidarity community" (and – since the participants do not know each other – as a compulsory solidarity community). A special feature of solidarity is that its organizing principle is "communistic", so contributions (shouldering the burden) are "ability" based (ability to pay), while the benefits provided are "needs" based. The balance between income and expenditure was often not considered to be important (when state pension systems started, they embraced a small circle, and there were no declared pension contributions), then – as the system became more widespread – this was regarded as something to be achieved in the short term.[18] The horizons of the system – in terms of its equilibrium – gradually expanded.

Solidarity and Correctness

When we talk about pension systems, sooner or later we always bump into the term "solidarity". Many people are of the opinion that this is the essence of pension systems – that it is simultaneously a need and a value. If we translate solidarity into the language of economics, we have perforce to use the word redistribution. According to this, the solidarity of pension systems is nothing other than the redistribution of income from those who have an "excess" of it in the direction of those who suffer a shortage of it. The main directions of solidarity-based redistribution are:

- from those with higher incomes to those with lower incomes (this is usually done through the regressive scale of changing income to pension entitlement in the benefit defined pay-as-you-go systems)
- from men to women (by disregarding mortality differences when determining the level of pension, or possibly applying a lower retirement age to women).

The opposite of solidarity is the stochastic individual equivalence of payments made into and benefits received from the system. Since the remaining life expectancy always remains uncertain – and even whether someone receives benefits at all after all his contribution payments is uncertain – so equivalence can only be fulfilled on a stochastic basis. In private life insurance, the condition of individual equivalence is self-evident. Since the necessary premium (individually equivalent to receiving one unit of benefit) is calculated by actuaries in insurance companies, the English literature on the subject refers to the individual equivalence of benefits and premiums as "actuarially fair". Following the Hungarian literature on the subject, we will be using this term in the same way, or sometimes simply in the short form "correct".

Realizing actuarial fairness means and requires precise accounting, and the equal treatment of members of the risk community in the correct (fair) sense that no member of the risk community has the right to systematically (i.e. not depending on the random variable representing the length of life) receive benefits from any other member, and is under no obligation to give this kind of benefit to others. Equivalence rules out the possibility of income transfer (not risk based) between genders, generations, social classes, etc.

If we examine how well actuarial fairness is actually enforced in practice, we find that, in social security pension systems, it is only present in trace form, whereas in private life insurance it has a strong presence, but is still not 100 percent. In private life insurance, the logic of competition keeps insurers to correct premium calculation; but this can only be achieved in so far as they know what factors influence the remaining life expectancy and to what extent. It is also important that the factors taken into account in premium pricing must be well measurable. These issues mean that we can split actuarial fairness into a theoretical and a practical concept. The theoretical concept serves as a goal and a standard measure, and the practical concept shows the degree to which it is possible at all to be correct. Henceforth, unless explicitly stated otherwise, we refer to actuarial fairness or correctness in its practical sense.

Actuarial fairness rules out redistribution, so this is the opposite of solidarity. We say this despite the fact that solidarity can also be interpreted in a wider sense. In this case, organizing a risk community generally is regarded as a solidaristic act – saying that (e.g. in the case of annuity insurance) those dying later than average receive an annuity from the reserve of those dying sooner than average. We refuse to interpret solidarity in as wide a sense as this, and only non-risk-based redistribution will be regarded as such.

Those opposed to the principle of actuarial fairness sometimes talk about "perverse" redistribution in relation to the functioning of market-based annuities. According to their logic, there is in these annuities a systematic flow of capital from persons in a worse financial condition to people in a better financial condition, since financial status correlates well with remaining life expectancy, yet this factor is not taken into account in the course of annuity premium calculation. So the premiums calculated as actuarially fair are, in reality, not correct. To be sure, this line of reasoning must remain on the agenda. It is a problem that must be tackled in the future for annuities calculated in an actuarially fair way.

We are of the opinion that both solidarity (primarily in the general sense) and correctness have an important function and place in the pension system. But we also think it important to distinguish clearly the effects of both: if we muddle these two things (which do not belong together), they will impair one another's effect – and, in the end, the effectiveness of the whole pension system. Our solution is to build solidarity and correctness separately, as different pillars of the pension system. Solidarity is inserted into Pillar 0, and correctness into all the others. There are currently major tasks to be undertaken in both areas. Pillar 0 does not exist at present, and the other pillars are far removed from even the practical interpretation of correctness. How can correctness be enforced in the current pillars, especially in the first, pay-as-you-go type pillar? To get the answer, we should take a step back in time.

The traditional systems of security were designed to "handle crisis". Their operation is well described by the term "solidaristic". The essence of solidarity in these cases was that certain people would step in to fill certain functions in case of need (the uncle would raise the orphan child; the child or grandchild would provide for parents and grandparents who had outlived their ability to work, etc. – if necessary). As the first great social security systems took over this model, their functioning can also be described as permanent crisis handling at the organization level. This is also true of the pay-as-you-go system. But the life-long contribution payment in itself brought regularity to these systems, and this, in itself, is contrary to crisis handling. The benefits they will receive as pensioners are built into the anticipations of those people who pay contributions for the greater part of their lives, and the pension they receive can be compared to the contributions paid and deemed to be too much or too little. This brings with it an increased demand for precise accounting from members (mostly from consistent payers, who pay well and over a long time). This also means a growing need to consider the subject of the system to be each individual, rather than the "population" generally.

Meanwhile this need has also been confirmed conceptually. Life-cycle theories and a life-cycle approach have emerged on the theoretical side, and the spread of private insurance has shown the "masses" the potential of precise accounting. Solidarity continues to remain a required and "popular" feature of the great social security systems, but the need to have it as an all-pervasive feature is increasingly coming into question, and there is a growing demand to have the need for solidarity defined precisely and its price determined exactly. This parallels the trend whereby individuals – as their well-being and personal property grow – feel less and less defenceless, more capable of "standing on their own two feet", and much less in need of being "cared for" by the state.

The efforts made to achieve individual accounting also mean that the need for differentiation has taken the place of the earlier need for levelling. Differentiation has to be based on the actual contributions and the actual risks. This tendency likewise parallels the growing wealth of the population, as people feel less need for levelling. (This trend is less clear in the current Hungarian situation, since in Hungary, the recent past has meant the greater part of the population became poorer rather than wealthier. This also means that the bulk of the population of Hungary has different, partly contradictory, requirements of the pension system.)

The need for differentiation and individual accounting also means that the field of defined benefit systems, which have solidarity[19] as a "built-in feature", is being cut back in many places, while defined contribution (DC) systems are burgeoning. Since DC systems are, by their very nature, funded, so funded systems are flourishing (in fact, so closely bound together are the concepts that DC systems may well be carrying all before them *because* they are funded).[20]

Thus enforcing correctness means that, from the defined benefit pay-as-you-go systems, we must gradually arrive at a funded, defined contribution system. An in-between step in this process could be (at least, this is the step we propose) a defined contribution pay-as-you-go system that will be explicitly funded later on.

The word "explicit" in front of funding is important, since, in our view (and this will be discussed further in this chapter), it is wrong (and it stirs up unnecessary dispute) to ask whether the funded system is better or worse than the pay-as-you-go system, since the pay-as-you-go system is also funded (only implicitly). A better question is: how should we design a correct pension system?

Placing the question of correctness at the centre of the debate may well be seen by some as simple moralizing, and far removed from a dry, economic line of reasoning. But the important thing (and something that can readily be grasped by economists) is that a correct pension system – and moreover *any* correct system – is economically *always* balanced – both in the short and in the long term. This is one of the most important economic requirements. Being just a little extreme, we might say that problems of balance may stem either from a bad economy or from unfairness, so in unbalanced cases it is always worth examining whether the given system is correct or not.

Finally we should mention a strange phenomenon: that those opposed to transforming Pillar I into an actuarially fair subsystem often raise their protests in the name of "fairness".[21] Of course, by "fairness" they do not mean the same thing as we mean by "correctness". According to their arguments, it would be "unfair" to transform the present system for the following reasons:

- The transformation will have winners and losers, and the transformation is unfair to the losers.
- Because of the transformation, there will be uncertainty as to the size of the anticipated pension, since that depends on changes in the remaining life expectancy.

- Moreover, it is *especially* unfair that, because the remaining life expectancy will probably gradually increase, the level of the pension will have to fall.

We think that these changes are justified. The losers in the transformation have, up until now, been the winners from an unfair situation. Ending an unfair situation should not in itself be regarded as a loss, even if, at an individual level, it may be. The decrease in the expected pension on account of increased life expectancy can also be easily defended and justified. The main point is: if someone belongs to a generation whose life expectancy increases compared to the previous generation, then his generation is healthier; ergo it should be expected to have a longer active phase, and consequently a higher retirement age. And the higher retirement age will "reinstate" the expected pension. (Of course, this highlights the incidental requirement that the retirement age should be much more flexible than it currently is.)

The Pension System and Individual Motivation

A certain logic has brought the state pension system to the stage it is at. But we could have arrived here along a different path, namely by looking at the inner problems of traditional security systems. One reason why traditional security systems declined is that the solidarity burdens were shifted – randomly and very unequally – onto certain members of the community. Thus there was a tendency among potential "sponsors" to seek to escape their liabilities, or to disperse the load across a wider circle and more equally. (So even in these systems the need for individual equivalence – which has nowadays become such a strong demand in state-controlled systems – made an appearance, albeit in an embryonic and unconscious way.)

Pension systems always express the motivations of the participants; moreover the system and the motivations mutually define each other. The "obligatory" feature of a pension system (if indeed the system has such a feature) encapsulates two notions: on the one hand that the citizens plan only for the short term, and do not save enough to cover their future needs; and on the other hand, that the community is unwilling to leave the "indolent" to look after themselves in their old age, but nevertheless wants to avoid this burden becoming too large. Wherever employer-organized pension systems are widespread, people envisage a career in a stable company, with a long stint at the same company. Wherever the system is funded, people place their faith in their own economic performance; while unfunded systems (mostly state organized) suggest a certain lack of self-confidence.

When someone (e.g. in Hungary) is offered the choice between different types of pension systems (or indeed of choosing a pension system at all), and he chooses the state-organized system, then by doing so he is basically placing his faith in the largest company in Hungary – the Hungarian state. He believes that while the players on the capital market might go bankrupt, the state cannot. He believes this to be so because the Hungarian state is larger than the other players and has more assets at its disposal. We think that in Hungarian professional circles today this opinion of the Hungarian state is very widespread. But in our view, this opinion is also somewhat outdated, since in the European Union there are larger (and more stable) enterprises, and the assets of the state will generally contract. Today, even state bankruptcy is not inconceivable – and not just in poor countries with bad governance! We believe that, when it comes to pensions, diversification is a better policy than "staking everything on one card".

It is very important for individuals that the pension system is transparent – that they can see what benefits they can expect to receive from it in the long term. The defined benefit systems provide this transparency at once. The disciples of the defined benefit system use this feature to attack defined contribution systems, claiming that that system does not allow individuals the opportunity to do their sums in advance. We think that this kind of comparison of the two systems is false and misguided in many respects, namely:

1. Defined contribution systems can also be calculated, only the calculation is not performed as simply – in a "naïve", single-step way – as in the case of the defined benefit system, but requires two steps: first, the projected capital has to be calculated, and then the projected annuity table has to be consulted – hardly an overly complicated task. In the defined contribution system, projection of the capital is neither more complicated nor more uncertain than the projection of entitlements in the defined benefit system, and the population trends that form the basis of the annuity table are relatively stable, or the changes occur slowly, so that the defined contribution pension is no more uncertain than the defined benefit pension, which is also modified from time to time for the same reasons.

2. The calculability of the defined benefit pension has always been relative, and has primarily meant a nominal calculability. In spite

of periodic attempts, the real-value calculability has never been a stable feature of the system.

3. The higher the pension is, or the less the pension is the main source of income, the less important calculability becomes.

Problems Associated with the Pay-as-You-Go System

The majority of problems associated with pension systems have to do with most prevalent system – the pay-as-you-go system – so we shall discuss these problems in more detail.

What Does the Term "Pay-as-You-Go System" Mean?

The first problem that must be cleared up is the term itself. Exactly what does "pay-as-you-go" cover? What is its opposite? Funded systems are usually regarded as the opposite of the pay-as-you-go system, but:

1. How do we handle partially funded systems? These are not pay-as-you-go, but what do we call them?
2. As we will see, pay-as-you-go systems can be regarded as having implicit state debt behind them, where payments into the system are used to purchase state bonds. In this sense, then, these systems are also totally funded – with the money invested exclusively in a special type of instrument!

In what follows, we shall use the term "pay-as-you-go system" in two senses – a narrow sense and a broad one.

1. In the narrow sense (or later on: "pure pay-as-you-go system") a pay-as-you-go system is a risk-handling system, sometimes also called a "claims dividing system". According to this, current claims are divided among the current members of the risk community. If we are speaking of pensions, then this means that the amount of contribution payments collected from the current contribution payers is equal to the amount required to pay the current pensions – neither more nor less.
2. In the wider sense, all state-organized pension systems are called pay-as-you-go systems, where implicit state debt covers the state liabilities to some extent.

The "everyday" terminology bounces to and fro between these two senses, and this is also what we intend to do. Where it is important, we will indicate the sense in which the term is being used (but it will generally be in the wider sense).

The wider sense also includes partially funded systems – i.e. systems where certain long-term reserves are used to equalize fluctuations, irrespective of whether these reserves are invested purely in state bonds[22] or in mixed products. At the same time, the extent of implicit state debt behind a pay-as-you-go system is uncertain if the rules of the pension system are not defined for a long time in advance. In this case, it is uncertain what the state guarantees (the starting level of pension, or only that there will always be such a system, so that pensioners will always receive some kind of pension).

The Pay-as-You-Go System and Correctness

In traditional pay-as-you-go systems, it is very difficult to examine the question of correctness – partly because they have a strong supporting function, and partly because, in the name of short-term financial balance, there are always different transfers between generations. In a certain sense, this opaqueness on the part of the system is also unfair. Naturally one can imagine pay-as-you-go systems where supporting functions are separated from other elements of the system. In this case, the picture is clearer, but usually income transfer between generations is still significant.

The pure pay-as-you-go system almost inevitably contains income transfer between generations, so the system creates winner and loser generations. Only in the theoretically possible scenario (with virtually 0 percent probability) when the population is in a steady state – that is, when the number of lives and the activity level of the individual age groups is the same from generation to generation – and when the economy is in a state of permanent growth, is there is no income transfer. If the pension level is fixed, and if the necessary contribution level is determined on the basis of this fixed pension level, then it will fluctuate depending on how the number of lives in the current pensioner population compares to the number of active people within the population. If someone belongs to a larger active age group that has to provide for a smaller pensioner population, then his contributions will be relatively smaller; if the demographic situation is reversed by the time he gets old, then his pension will be provided at the cost of a much higher level of contributions from those active at the time. So, as a pensioner, he will receive benefits that he did not earn when he was young. If, on the other hand, we fix the contribution level, then the resulting pension will fluctuate as the ratio of active to inactive changes. In this case – i.e. in the case of the pure pay-as-you-go system – repayment of the implicit state debt behind the pay-as-you-go system depends on demographic chance, and the implicit debt taken on by relatively larger generations is paid (partly) by the relatively smaller generations. In pay-as-you-go systems in the narrower sense, the contribution payments made by an individual during his life cycle and the benefits received from the system by the same individual bear little relationship to one another, so the system is not correct in this sense.

The status of the implicit state debt behind pay-as-you-go systems is uncertain in many respects, since the state does not usually handle it in this way. The implicit state debt – as we shall see – is in many ways only a construct, derived from the guarantees and liabilities undertaken by the state. The (hopefully) theoretical threat exists that the state could renege on these guarantees. A good opportunity to do this would be to terminate the system from one day to the next (since terminating a pay-as-you-go system from one day to the next is as easy as introducing the system from one day to the next). In such a case (we emphasize that this is only theoretical, but all the same it is conceivable), the generations that would lose the most are those that are on the brink of retirement – those that have not yet received any benefits from the system, but that have paid contributions all their lives. The generations to win the most would be those that received benefits when the system was introduced without having previously contributed. This is the extreme case (and unfairness) of transfer between generations. But to detect unfairness we do not necessarily have to assume the system is scrapped. It is enough if we suppose a demographic situation that is constantly deteriorating, from generation to generation, with the number of active people steadily falling and the proportion of current pensioners steadily rising (though, of course, their absolute number is also decreasing!). It is then possible that ultimately the last active generation is so small that it cannot pay any pension to the last retired pensioner generation – to those people who have regularly paid, throughout their lives, the continuously increasing contribution!.

As far as correctness is concerned, we have to nail an important, well-known principle that – interestingly – has not really been used yet in relation to pension systems. The principle is this: "there is no such thing as a free lunch!" Someone is bound to pay. And, in the words of another well-known proverb, "he who pays the piper, calls the tune". One of the most important objections to the literature that defends the pay-as-you-go system is that this point does not even appear. When the defenders of the pay-as-you-go system compare it to funded systems, then they work out criteria for examining which demographic conditions are more favourable to one or the other system. But the important question is actually whether the system is correct or not. If, thanks to favourable demographic trends, one generation receives more benefits than are justified on the basis of that generation's contribution payments, that does not mean (or is not proof) that the pay-as-you-go system is better than the funded; in this case, in reality the state takes out a loan (implicitly) that will have to be paid back by a later generation. And this is a serious unfairness!

When, after World War II, many funded systems found their reserves had been bombed out, yet the state kept on paying pensions all the same (i.e. introduced the pay-as-you-go system), then in reality the state created an implicit state debt that it has forgotten to pay back. In the 1960s there were supposedly debates about the funding of the system, but these were abandoned on the pretext that people had lost faith in funded systems because the capital behind those systems could so easily be swept away by inflation, war or economic depression. Conversely, the argument went, the pay-as-you-go system functions well, the people are satisfied with it, and they don't want change.[23]

This argument was possible in an environment that did not contain the concept of implicit state debt, where people thought that the funded system was the opposite of the pay-as-you-go system. In reality – as we have already seen – the pay-as-you-go system is a special kind of funded system that has exclusively (implicit) state debt as the capital behind it. So the right question is not whether the system is funded or pay-as-you-go, but whether to pay back the implicit state debt or roll it forwards (and increase it). The decision was made to roll it forward, which brings with it the problem that the debt taken on by one generation was shifted onto the next generation. And this is a serious problem for correctness: since, in reality, this criterion concerns not just a generation but each of its members, then, as a minimum, correctness requires that a generation should arrange for the debts it has taken on. This way of operating a pay-as-you-go system is – in improving demographic conditions – nothing more than institutionally rolling debt forward to later generations. And when the demographic conditions are unfavourable, those generations that had nothing to do with creating the debt will have to begin paying it back.

Traditional Arguments on the Side of the Pay-as-You-Go System

The intellectual support for the pay-as-you-go system in Hungary is very strong. Since unfairness is "built into" the system and, as we shall see, there are other problems with it, this is somewhat surprising. We can discern two levels of reasons for the phenomenon: on the upper level there are the moral attitudes, and on the lower level there are the formal/rational arguments.

The moral attitude of the supporters of the pay-as-you-go system is largely (though not exclusively) aligned with what we could call the "political left". The key words here are: solidarity, support for those in need, social equality, non-profit functioning, etc. A characteristic feature of its proponents is that, following the socialist writers of the 19th century, they see the main problems of society in capital, economic rationality, economic competition and profit-oriented functioning (which are all basic economic concepts, and without which – as we now know – the economy cannot function at all). When it comes to easing these problems, they prefer the great remedy of the 20th century – state intervention and redistribution. Thus, those people who hold this moral attitude are open to all arguments that use the words so dear to them, and are automatically suspicious of arguments that use the despised vocabulary. They – unconsciously – select between arguments, thirsting for those that support their basic moral position and seeking to disprove those that counter it.[24] The initial versions of the pay-as-you-go system were filled with solidaristic elements: organized by the state on a non-profit basis; no competition in it; nothing to do with the business world. So all its features arouse pleasant sensations in the politically left-oriented brain. And the disciples of the funded system use the very terms (capital, competition, profit, etc.) that they regard as the root cause of the problems.

Let us look at two important arguments that are very popular, but that do not stand up to more rigorous examination.

Argument one: The pay-as-you-go system is cheaper than the funded system.

Interestingly, little effort has gone into proving this argument, as it seems so obvious. It is usually demonstrated by comparing the annual administration cost of the pay-as-you-go system, projected onto the annual contributions, against the annual functioning expenses of the pension funds, projected onto the annual payments or the capital. What usually emerges is that the value is smaller in the case of the pay-as-you-go system, so the conclusion is obvious: this system is cheaper (and consequently better) than the funded system. Unfortunately, this argument is problematic because:

1. The things compared are not necessarily comparable.
2. The services provided and the benefits behind the two types of expenditure ares not the same.
3. It does not take into account certain hidden expenses.
4. The contribution payer and the annuitant are separated, so the comparison is problematic for any given generation.

Comparison of the cost of the pay-as-you-go and the funded system is no easy matter. For example currently in Hungary the pay-as-you-go system is operated through several institutions. Contributions are collected by APEH (Hungarian Tax and Financial Supervising Office), while collecting the data necessary to determine the pension, calculating and granting the pension are the tasks of ONYF (Central Administration of National Pension Insurance). So expenses are borne by those two organizations plus the employers. In addition, many experts are of the opinion that the costs of the pension fund sector are higher than is reasonable. But the underlying benefits and services are also different. We might mention that many pay-as-you-go systems seem cheap compared to the funded system because they do not keep exact records, as a funded system must. Nowadays, however, there is an increasing requirement on the part of the pay-as-you-go system to keep records, so this advantage will disappear.

From a different angle: the pay-as-you-go system does not build up reserves, so those do not have to be managed. (This is only true currently, when the number of recipients are greater than the number of payees.) Obviously, then, there is no expense associated with this aspect of fund management. But it is problematic to apportion the expenses of fund management to the pension system, as it is something that follows naturally from maintaining the fund and provides good returns.

And finally, the implicit state debt behind the pay-as-you-go system bears interest – albeit in an implicit way! This interest has to be paid by taxpayers, which would not be the case if their money earned interest in true investments. This hidden, fund-proportional (i.e. having a base much greater than the annual income) expense factor, which is the equivalent of several percent, has never been taken into account by pay-as-you-go systems – even though, in a mature system such as Hungary's, the amount involved is comparable to the total annual contribution.[24] The imprecise accounting of the state debt behind the system is neither justifiable, nor sustainable in the long term.

The "cheapness" of the system as an argument is thus based on largely exaggerated evidence. In all probability, not only is it not true, but it could be very far from reality. From time to time some adherents of the pay-as-you-go system also sense this and wheel out a well-refined version of the above argument. It runs thus: it is not worth exchanging a well-functioning pay-as-you-go system for a funded one, because the costs of the transition would be far too large, and not worth it.

The problem with this argument is that, whichever way you look at it, a start must be made in repaying the implicit state debt behind the pay-as-you-go system – in favourable demographic conditions in the name of correctness, and in unfavourable demographic conditions so that the current contribution payers have at least some hope of receiving the annuity due to them later. And this cannot be done within the pay-as-you-go system, since the state cannot properly manage a portfolio containing debt that is not its own. Secondly, the administration of the pay-as-you-go system also has to be overhauled, so the system badly needs "transition". Thirdly, transition to a funded system at the level of society creates the totally new, beneficial function of fund management, which should not be regarded as an expense, but rather as an investment that will bring a return (not to mention the fact that this is not even an investment by the state, so the state has absolutely no expense in relation to transition).

The second argument, below, is rather more defensive, seeking as it does to neutralize the attacks coming from the side of the funded system. These thrusts contend that the funded system is better, because the savings behind the system are invested (which stimulates and drives forward the whole economy), whereas the pay-as-you-go system has no such economic benefits.

Argument two. This is not true, because the implicit state debt behind the pay-as-you-go system is embodied in implicit investments that the state has made using this source, and from which the whole economy benefits.

At first glance it would seem that neither the proof nor the refutation of this argument is simple. In fact, however, knowing as we do that pay-as-you-go systems were largely introduced because the capital behind funded systems was destroyed, and considering that the implicit state debt has been accumulated because, when the system was introduced, contribution payments were not invested, but were paid out as annuities (and certainly used for consumption), it is quite simple to disprove! There is, though, one thing that makes the argument partly true: there might have been periods in the existence of pay-as-you-go systems when contribution payments exceeded annuity benefits. In these periods the state "stole" this excess, and might have used it for these implicit investments. Or not? Who knows? What is certain is that, if there were such implicit investments, they were several orders of magnitude smaller than the implicit capital.[25]

On the subject of the relationship between the pay-as-you-go system and economic policy, we must make the point that any economic policy that favours the pay-as-you-go system presupposes a political leadership that views the state as the biggest economic actor – that is, in competition with the others – and thus reinforces the state's quasi-monopolistic position. The requirement of funding, on the other hand, diminishes the role of the state, so funded systems tend to be introduced and operated in environments where there is a liberal approach to the state.

Pay-as-you-go systems are generally proposed in mixed systems on account of their stability, even by supporters of the funded pension system. As one of the pillars of a multi-pillar system, it fulfils a "mitigating" function (i.e. it guarantees a part of the pension). On the other hand, achievement of stability does not necessarily entail operating a pay-as-you-go system: stability can also be ensured by derivatives (e.g. issued by the state). The apparently wholesale support for the pay-as-you-go system is partly explained by a reluctance on the part of advocates of the funded system to leave themselves too exposed.

The general point might also be made that, when the pay-as-you-go system is contrasted with the funded system, the models contrasted contain several features that are not necessarily closely associated, yet it is claimed that the features are only conceivable in those combinations. In reality, the situation is rather different, and the features of the models can be combined fairly freely. As an example, stability can be solved in the funded system with derivatives, and a pay-as-you-go system can also be operated on a (partly) funded basis, although the absence of funding seems a particular feature of the state model.

The Pay-as-You-Go System as Unsolved Debt Crisis

The leading type of pension system in the world at present is the pay-as-you-go system. Its current commanding position has developed since World War II, and has come about in two distinct ways:
1. It was created this way originally (the only example of this is the USA).
2. The former funded system has "mutated into" the pay-as-you-go system (all others).

The system that was originally created as pay-as-you-go has seen an extension of the contribution-free state pension system to wide classes of society and the introduction of contribution payments. Its development in the United States was associated with economic depression.

The funded systems were converted into a pay-as-you-go system in the wake of the Second World War, when the greater part of their capital disappeared. So one might say that their development is also a crisis phenomenon.

However, not only is it the development, but also the continuous operation of pay-as-you-go systems that can be regarded as a crisis phenomenon – a kind of (well managed, but never solved) "debt crisis". Because – contrary to the primary logic of the pay-as-you-go system – it would be virtually impossible to terminate the system in such a way that the earned pension entitlements are also terminated along with the contribution payments. It is evident that the state must provide a guarantee, so the earned entitlements function as state debt. Thus a huge debt stock (implicit state debt) stands behind the pay-as-you-go system. The value of this is: the expected present value of the remaining annuity of current pensioners plus the capital value of the pension entitlements accumulated by those currently active. This debt was created at the inception of the pay-as-you-go system – and whenever it was extended – and it has been taken on largely by generations that have in the meantime "died out".[26] Repayment of the debt may become necessary as the demographic conditions deteriorate and the number of actives decreases; but advocates of the system usually give no thought to repayment, and take it for granted that the debt stock will be rolled forward from generation to generation. This is problematic for three reasons (which is why we call the pay-as-you-go system a permanent, unsolved debt crisis):

1. As we stated earlier, under unfavourable demographic conditions repayment of the debt will, in the end, fall to an active generation that had nothing to do with its accumulation. The system is, then, morally problematic – one can say that unfairness is built into the system.

2. The generation of current pensioners and those approaching retirement are dependent on the decision by those currently active to maintain the social consensus that allowed the current pensioners to roll forward the debt in their active ages. The smaller the number of active and the larger the number of pensioners, the greater the temptation to scrap the rolled debt (or a large part of it) without repayment (when, regardless of the earned entitlements, pensions are not paid, or their value is greatly reduced).

3. When a country becomes an open one, and the national economy gradually disappears (globalization!) it will become more and more difficult to define at all who belongs to the system on the active side, while the earned entitlements will probably remain quite well documented. So this objective and positive process will prevent the state from being indebted in the long term.

The pay-as-you-go system is not only a crisis phenomenon, but is also a uniquely bad method of resolving the crisis, since the worst way to manage a debt is to roll it forward indefinitely. If we divide the annuity payment into capital and interest payments, then above a term of approximately 15 years the ratio of capital payments becomes infinitesimal, even at a relatively low interest rate. In other words: it is not worth having a debt for longer than this. No matter how big the debt mountain, if a country is able to pay the interest, it only has to "work a little harder" to start repaying the capital, too; and the reward for this "harder work" is to be felt just a few years down the road – in a decreasing interest burden and, later, in a shrinking total debt mountain.[27]

The Missing "Protection Ring"

The pay-as-you-go system performs well in times of a crisis. But once the crisis is past (with reconstruction and less social discontent), there is no reason to maintain it, since society is thus depriving itself of a "protection ring". A funded system can ultimately "fall into" a pay-as-you-go system; but what can the pay-as-you-go system "fall into"? If there is enough accumulated capital, and no debt, then losing a large part of it is not nearly as big a problem as it would be if the accumulated debt matched the capital. So the pay-as-you-go system should be reserved for what it is: a crisis management tool for (at most) one or two decades, for extraordinary, unanticipated turns of events. The generation that introduces a pay-as-you-go system should, if possible, *itself* aim to repay the debt it has taken on. It could also be said that pay-as-you-go systems are the protective "rear guard" of funded systems. From this it also follows that, once the crisis has passed, the system should be funded as soon as possible, so the protective rear guard is established again.

The advocates of the pay-as-you-go system usually declare it a safe system, unlike the funded system, which could, as history has shown, lose its capital. But unfortunately, pay-as-you-go systems are even more vulnerable and defenceless, since, in case of state bankruptcy, pensioners are left totally unprotected. State bankruptcy has always seemed only a theoretical possibility, and so it has never been taken too seriously. But recent events have shown that state bankruptcy is *not* merely a theoretical possibility. We might also speculate that the more liabilities we place on the state, the less it will be immune to bankruptcy.

The Explicit Funding of Pay-as-You-Go Systems

But why do pay-as-you-go systems have to be explicitly funded? How can they be made correct? How can this be achieved gradually? Let us examine these questions in turn.

Funding basically means that the state repays the implicit state debt, and the reserves of the pension system are placed in other instruments later on – possibly none in state bonds. But why does the state debt have to be repaid in the first place? The answer *should* be obvious. Nevertheless, experience shows that it is not. Many people believe that it is possible, indeed desirable, to roll the state debt forward into infinity. However, a fresh tendency could be observed in some developed countries in the late 1990s – moreover one that, in places, has even entered legislation: to balance the government budget and repay state debt. We might say that – in those countries at least – common sense has at last prevailed! What is the reason behind this trend?

Being Covered, Implicit State Debt

In the sections above, we have referred several times to the "implicit state debt", but we have not explained in detail what it really means, and what the associated problems are. The *implicit* state debt is implicit, or hidden, because it does not feature on the state balance sheet, and most people (in this instance, it is primarily the decision makers that are important) do not even know of its existence. The whole thing is that the pension entitlements accumulated in the pay-as-you-go system are, ultimately, the liabilities of the state – and thus the debt of the state. In a mature pay-as-you-go system, everybody with a pension entitlement will have earned this through earlier contribution payments (or are earning it now), and the very first generation of annuitants, who received an annuity without contribution payments (or whose reserves were destroyed in the war) will already have died out. On account of the accumulated entitlements, then, it is practically impossible for the state to scrap the system, saying "from now on there will be no contribution payments, and nor will we be paying annuities". And so it is impossible to eliminate the implicit state debt at a blow.

The existence of the implicit state debt is well covered by the pure pay-as-you-go system. There is a tendency for non-pure pay-as-you-go systems to be regarded as theoretically pure systems, and viewed as if the rules of a pure pay-as-you-go system applied to them, too. In pure pay-as-you-go systems, the income is always equal to the expenditure, suggesting that everything is in order. The existence of the state debt is only revealed if we ask the question: what would happen if contribution payments ceased tomorrow? The answer is that, due to the existing entitlements, payment would have to be continued, only its source would be other state income – which means that repayment of the implicit state debt would have to be started. Of course, this question is usually not asked, and so the debt remains hidden.

What adds to the confusion is that – as we have already seen – there are generally[28] two functions mixed up in pay-as-you-go systems: the pension system and a support system. So only part of the contributions paid generates entitlements; another part goes to indigents who have not earned entitlements. But these two parts are usually not clearly separated.

It is an inner tendency of pay-as-you-go systems to keep precise records of entitlements and gradually to make benefit payments independent of the actual contribution income, i.e. to terminate the pure pay-as-you-go system. This comes about largely in deteriorating demographic conditions, when a large active generation looks uneasily at the succeeding small generation and starts to wonder whether it will be capable of paying the annuity that the older generations have earned through their contribution payments. In a deteriorating demographic situation the answer is clearly no: in this case the contribution will not be enough to pay the earned pensions, since the possible contribution level also has a kind of upper limit. Then again, if the contribution level is raised anyway, the next generation has an even greater pension entitlement, so the implicit state debt grows, etc.

It is also an inner tendency – likewise related to the tendency to record and take account of pension entitlements – for the pension and support functions of the pay-as-you-go system to be gradually separated.

In what follows, let us suppose that the pension and support systems have been separated, and that pension entitlements are precisely recorded. For this, the most plausible[29] method is to convert the pension system into a fund account system and organize the support function independently of this (naturally, it is independent only in a relative sense).

This way we arrive at a (not pure) pay-as-you-go system that is already purely a pension system, where contribution payments and the earned entitlements are precisely recorded on individual interest-earning accounts, and where the annuity is proportional to the balance of the individual account, and naturally depends on the remaining life expectancy of the individual at retirement. After this, the annuity is paid by decreasing the individual account; the current retired annuitants form a risk community, in which the account balance of the deceased is always divided between the accounts of those still living, and in this way every account lasts until the death of its owner, no matter how long he lives (even if the annuity payments would long ago have depleted the original account balance).

In this case, the sum of the (not so) implicit state debt is the balance of the individual accounts. It frequently happens that the contribution payments and the annuity benefits of a given year are not the same. What should we do with the difference?

If contribution payments exceed the value of annuity benefits, then the system produces a surplus, which is invested prudently, as it will certainly be needed later on. If the state takes away this surplus without giving anything in return, then the implicit state debt to be repaid later is increased by this amount. If the state takes it away and issues state bonds instead, then the stock of debt behind the pension system also grows, but instead of being purely implicit, it becomes a partly explicit state debt. If it is invested in instruments other than those issued by the state (e.g. stock or foreign state bonds), then the surplus does not increase the state debt. But a surplus is probably a rare and atypical phenomenon, since recording of precise individual accounts is in itself usually a requirement that reflects deteriorating demographic conditions. So contribution income will typically be below annuity payments.

If annuities exceed contributions, then the state has to pay the difference from other sources. What actually happens in this case is that a portion of the implicit state debt expires, and the state has to repay it. Since a pure pension system that records entitlements only has legitimacy if the level of contributions is derived from the pensions to be paid in the future, rather than from the currently payable pension liabilities, increasing the contribution level can be ruled out as a possibility.

The Desirable Level of State Debt

In many respects, the state debt behaves the same way as any other debt. When someone takes on a loan, he expands his current horizons at the expense of his future horizons (when the loan has to be repaid). If someone takes out a loan, he can live better than his current financial situation would allow. If he dies before the loan is repaid, then the debt passes to his heirs; repayment of the loan and the interest then narrows their horizons, even though they never had the original loan to expand them in the first place.[30]

The same is true of state debt. If a generation takes on a loan, and this increases the state debt, then that generation can spend more, in the knowledge that later on the burden of repaying the loan and the interest will curtail its possibilities. If that generation only pays the interest and does not repay the loan (or, what is even worse, fails even to pay the interest, adding it to the original debt), but instead rolls it forward, then repayment of the total debt is "shifted" to the next generation, which inherits the liability without having enjoyed the advantages of taking out the loan.

And the same is true of *implicit* state debt. Let us suppose that it was created in the aftermath of World War II, when the accumulated capital of the funded pension systems was destroyed in bombing (or rather the assets that embodied this capital). What happened then was that the credit of the current pensioners (and those approaching pension age, who had already paid into the system) objectively ceased. In the name of social solidarity, the state took on a debt, and paid a (support-like) pension – out of solidarity – to these people. The method of the debt was implicit, so the pension contributions of the active were not accumulated for them – only entitlements were recorded – and in this way the state objectively began to increase the implicit state debt, without embarking on a programme to decrease it. Since this went on for generations, today's generations have inherited a great stock of debt, but have received nothing from the original "loan". The current generations may continue rolling forward this state debt, but the interest on it still has to be paid – which in itself is unfair, since what business of theirs is the old debt? Of course, the interest payments come from taxes (contributions – but that is irrelevant here).

The conclusion must be that rolling the state debt forward means encumbering future generations with our burdens. Just because we also inherited it in the same way, is an insufficient reason not to resolve the problem.

Naturally, there is here a very important difference between explicit and implicit state debt: a generation that has inherited implicit state debt, and plans to roll it forward, would do better first to make the debt explicit. The explicit state debt then has to be repaid at all costs (or at least it is very hard and very dangerous not to pay it back); in the case of implicit debt, it is quite easy just to "sit tight" (as a number of examples show). Even stipulating repayment by law does not help, as laws can always be changed. If, for example, a small active generation provides for a large pensioner population whose pensions are paid from the implicit and totally justified state debt, then the legislators (who are mostly members of the active age groups) could well start to cut back on the liabilities. It may well be that they have no choice, because, regardless of entitlements, tax income does not cover the payment of the implicit state debt[31] and its interest.

And we have not even really touched on such issues as the concept of the "state" itself becoming uncertain in the future. It is possible that, in the European Union, part of the liabilities of the current Hungarian state will be gradually transferred to a common "government". It is far from certain that this will acknowledge all implicit state debts (so today's generations really should not leave them implicit). With the free flow of labour, it becomes uncertain who exactly has to repay the debt; it is possible that the implicit debt is not repaid, because, all of a sudden, nobody can determine whom it refers to! For example, if it suddenly becomes normal for the active Hungarian population to go to work abroad and only to return home as pensioners. It could be that employees who come to Hungary in their place have a funded pension system behind them (in the country where they came from); since they will remain in that system, they will not pay contributions to the Hungarian pay-as-you-go pension system at all.

There Is No Need to Roll the State Debt Forward

Let us look now at a simple example. Suppose a state has 100 units of debt, and there is an interest rate of 10 percent. The state has no intention of repaying the debt, but it does pay interest correctly. In this case, the cash flow each year is as follows (the debt is indicated separately):

Table 57. Interest payable without capital repayment

Year	n	N+1	n+2	n+3	n+4	n+5	...
Debt	100	100	100	100	100	100	100
Interest paid	-10	-10	-10	-10	-10	-10	-10

If the state would only decide to repay just one unit of the debt each year, then this cash flow would change as follows:

Table 58. Interest payable with capital repayment

Year	n	n+1	n+2	n+3	n+4	n+5	n+6	n+7	n+8	n+9	n+10	...
Debt	100	99	98	97	96	95	94	93	92	91	90	...
Capital payment	-1	-1	-1	-1	-1	-1	-1	-1	-1	-1	-1	-1
Interest paid	-10	-9.9	-9.8	-9.7	-9.6	-9.5	-9.4	-9.3	-9.2	-9.1	-9.0	...
All payments	-11	-10.9	-10.8	-10.7	-10.6	-10.5	-10.4	-10.3	-10.2	-10.1	-10	...

The result is plain: for 10 years all payments are a little higher, but after that the payment is lower. Because a portion of the capital is even being repaid, the debt gradually decreases (although at this rate it only disappears totally in 100 years). Of course, after the tenth year, the proportion of capital repayment can be increased as the interest rate payments decrease.

To put it another way: let us examine, using an interest rate of 10 percent, what the ratio is between the capital and interest payments in the first year in the case of an annuity payment calculation over different terms.

Table 59. Ratio of payments as a function of the term

Term	Capital payment	Interest payment
5	62%	38%
10	39%	61%
15	24%	76%
20	15%	85%
25	9%	91%
30	6%	94%
35	4%	96%
40	2%	98%
45	1%	99%

It is clear that the longer the term, the higher is the ratio of interest payment in the total payment. At the infinite term (i.e. when the capital is not repaid at all) naturally the proportion of interest is 100 per cent. Of course, the level of interest rates also influences the above table. The higher the interest rate, the shorter the term when the capital payment reaches onq percent, and vice versa. The lesson to be learned is that it is not worth choosing a term too long, because the liability is there for a long time, and a lot of interest has to be paid. When the ratio of the capital payment is small, then it is worth shortening the term and increasing the total payment just a little, because, at the cost of an insignificant increase in total payment, the debt is repaid much sooner. Naturally, what should be avoided most is rolling forward the debt, when there is absolutely no repayment of the capital.

Accordingly, rolling forward the state debt is a bad policy in the long term. The state has unnecessary expenditure, of which it could – albeit only in the long term – entirely rid itself.

A Correct Pay-as-You-Go System. The Method of Funding

The only truly correct pay-as-you-go system is naturally a defunct pay-as-you-go system, since rolling forward the implicit state debt behind it is unfair towards the generations of the future. But – naturally – correctness has several levels, and from this perspective the systems can be compared with one another.

A correct pay-as-you-go system precisely records contribution payments, credits interest on these, and calculates the benefits according to these and the remaining life expectancy of the individual; throughout the annuity payment it earns proper interest on the capital, thus providing the annuity benefit, and it indexes the annuity accordingly.

Thus a correct pay-as-you-go system looks like any funded system – with the important difference that the reserves behind the system are state debt bonds, and appear as such on the pension accounts. This pay-as-you-go system is called the Notionally Defined Contribution (fund account) stetystem.

One of the most important features of a fund account system is that it makes the pay-as-you-go and the funded system comparable; moreover – since its basic structure is the same – it provides transferability between the two systems. Theoretically, this transferability could go in two directions, with transfer from the funded system to the fund account (i.e. pay-as-you-go) system also possible; but bearing in mind the above discussions, we shall leave this potentially dangerous notion in the realms of theory.

Creating transferability is a very important step, through this the pay-as-you-go system can be terminated relatively simply, gradually and largely voluntarily. By registering the fund accounts the implicit state debt has mostly become explicit (although the state may have to pass a law expressly stating that this must be accounted in the state balance sheet – but there are no obstacles in the way of this accounting practice). If, alongside the pay-as-you-go system, there is a second pillar that functions in a similar way, but that offers the choice of competing pension funds, which invest their clients' money on the capital markets, then the members of Pillar I (the fund account system) could be allowed without further ado to transfer voluntarily to Pillar II, and take their reserves with them. Of course, this reserve is state debt, but at this point it is formally "printed".

The state can only repay its debt if it is not in Pillar I, because repayment within Pillar I would mean that the state would have to invest on the capital market, which is best avoided. But it can repay debt transferred to Pillar II at the pace it pleases. If it chooses to repay slowly, then it can pass laws stipulating that pension funds should keep a certain percentage of their reserves in state bonds.[32] If it chooses faster repayment, then it repeals these laws, and does not appear in the money market with a supply of state bonds, thus making it impossible for pension funds to invest their clients' money in these papers.

The Possible Social Security Systems of the Future

Finally, let us take a look at a future that we think is achievable. It usually takes generations to change the social conditions and needs that form the basis of the pension system; so very often these appear in discussions as a self-evident, fixed backdrop. That said, the changes that affect the fundamentals of the social security system have now built up to the level where the framework of the system needs to be seriously overhauled. (Or at least such changes and reforms are on the horizon.)

The vastness of the social security system is the result – and the reflected image – of a special social and economic situation that is already behind us. The most important features of this bygone age are:

1. Mass production – mass insurance. Simple and cheap, inflexible standard solutions.
2. Typically one job for life, in the same profession. Large employers.
3. The individual typically stays in the same country all his life.
4. Most people are poor, without any significant property.
5. People are not used to caring for themselves – the state thinks (but doesn't "care") for them, forces them to look to the future, and organizes the institutions necessary for this.

By contrast, today:

1. Production has shifted to satisfy individual needs – also in the field of caring/self-care.
2. People change their jobs and type of work many times in their lives – thus they need flexible caring/self-caring systems.
3. Temporary international employment is becoming more and more common, and this also increases the need for flexible solutions. It is more and more difficult to define national economies (see our EU membership!).
4. The number of middle-class people with property is growing (although not so much "producing" property, such as stock, but rather "non-producing" property, such as an apartment or holiday home).
5. People's financial education is improving, their foresight is expanding, and this leads to a greater need for them to control their own destiny.
6. The sense of needing solidarity and the willingness to "offer" solidarity are decreasing, especially on the part of the wealthier.

Below we try to summarize the main characteristics and tendencies governing – we think – the development of the social security system (and primarily the pension system). These tendencies influence the way we think about the current tasks.

The core subject of the social security system is, more and more, becoming the individual; and the individual is increasingly providing for his retirement himself. In the case of those classes where it is "guaranteed" that they will not need the support of the community, the state will gradually withdraw and "let them out" of the risk community. This class is steadily growing. The role of the state is gradually changing. From provider, it is shifting to organizer and compeller of provision, and then to an informative institution that only provides the framework for self-care. The most important goal of the state as an information- and framework-providing institution will be to gradually eliminate the need for its own intervention, which will decrease as the wealth and future-planning consciousness of its citizens increase. The state will gradually withdraw to operating a support system for the most downtrodden (whose numbers will gradually dwindle). The role of the social security system will be taken over by private insurance and by accumulation of wealth.

While a social security system exists, different risks will be handled by separate subsystems. This means that disability, orphan's and retirement pension risks become separated from one another.

In the handling of risks, the principle of differentiation – that everyone should contribute according to his own risk and receive benefits from the system in proportion to his own contributions and his own risk – is becoming more effective. This will be accomplished, along with an increase in the value of benefits and income from other sources at retirement. Of course, this can only be based on an exact recording of contributions, broken down to the level of individuals.

The social security system will gradually become totally funded, with government securities missing from investments, because the state has no debt. Investments are not limited to Hungary, but, in order to spread the risk, are international. When it comes to investments, the state has a role in only one area: the government will maintain a fund-managing trustee to invest in market instruments. Up to the value of the fund handled by this organization, the state releases special government bonds (i.e. the net debt of the state is zero!) that have the feature of steady fixed long-term yield. The social security system uses this to cover the accounts of the poorest, thus making their pension calculable. The higher the expected pension, the more liberty the insured has to decide how to invest his pension fund – benefiting from excess yield achieved and bearing any losses.

From income- and property-proportional tax, the state operates a solidarity subsystem for the poorest. But the most important task of the state regarding solidarity is not to provide benefits, but to make the indigent capable of caring for themselves – with education, the provision of information, organizing – that is, to gradually eliminate the need for income redistribution.

Pensions are internationally portable, following the increasing number of employees who will build their careers in several countries. Contributions will be based less on wages, since income will depend less and less on wages (and more and more on capital income, entre-preneurial profit). The state will make possible irregular payments into the system, and furthermore, if a certain fund value is accumulated, the insured may suspend further payments. The insured, the employer, spouse, alo etc., can (voluntarily) make payments to the account, and the accounts can be inherited (according to specified rules). In this case, the account balance of the testator is added to the account of the inheritor.

Commencing to claim benefits is flexible, and the annuity can be suspended for longer or shorter periods of time. The insured can also request temporary withdrawals from the account. It becomes general practice for couples to unite their accounts and receive a two-person annuity. Regarding the annuity as well as the accumulation phase, the insured has a wide choice of provider organizations, both domestic and international.

Employment of the elderly will become common, and in this way the pension will be only one source of income for the elderly, and will become less and less significant. Pension is added to all other income, and the total is taxed.

Bearing all this in mind, claiming a pension will cease to be a general break in the life of the individual. Within certain boundaries (depend-ing primarily on the minimum annuity his fund can currently provide), the individual can choose freely when to start his "pension"; but this has nothing to do with whether he is working or not, or how much he is working.

A DESIRABLE PENSION SYSTEM

We hope that the facts discussed in the previous sections make it clear that society is forced to take steps to reform the pension system. We also believe that our conclusions, based on the arguments so far, are correct; that is, we suggest developing a system that is more "correct" in the actuarial sense than the current one. The years since the change in regime (1989) have demonstrated the need to create a more flexible system, and the demands of the coming decades make this need urgent. We accept some of the arguments of the defined benefit system that primarily support those modes of risk distribution between the individual and society that favour the individual, but fundamentally, we would like to argue on the side of defined contribution (DC) systems. The advantage of these DC systems is that they are flexible, and they also do not represent uncovered commitments (or liabilities of unknown duration). In summary, we favour an actuarially correct, defined contribution system.

From all that has been said, it is likewise clear that we favour (explicitly) funded systems over pay-as-you-go schemes. For us, though, reform of the pension system in Hungary cannot be "started from scratch": the first step must involve reform of the current system with its significant implicit state debt. So the system to be developed must follow in its logic the rules of a funded system, and possibly – if economic conditions in a few decades (or maybe sooner!) permit – pension promises can be partially bought out. It is also an argument in its favour that a system of this kind can readily be compared to Pillar II, the private pension funds. Comparing performance might even serve as an incentive for private pension funds to raise their yield, and in this way the effectiveness of other elements of the pension system may be improved. (In our view the system of institutions surrounding the second pillar also needs serious reform, as the present structure benefits neither the insured, nor the institutions.)

In the literature on the subject, the system that best satisfies the above conditions is the NDC (Notionally Defined Contribution) system. It was first proposed by George Buchanan in 1968. This system directly ties contribution payments to the annuity benefit provided, and defines the risk community within a given generation.

The main thrust of our proposition is that the first pillar should be transformed into an NDC system. To deal with the problems that the defined benefit system currently handles (and that a defined contribution system of course does not handle), and because "solidarity" can have only a very limited role in a defined contribution scheme, we suggest the introduction of a new Pillar 0 beside the two existing ones (or three, according to a different way of thinking).

The Main Goals of Transforming the Pension System

By way of introduction, we will try to define the principles and goals according to which we would like the pension system to be transformed. Of course, transformation is a lengthy process, and we will not discuss all the steps in this lengthy process in the same detail. We will discuss the first steps in more detail, and the later steps only briefly. But the principles and goals remain unchanged throughout. We believe that the pension system reforms must aim for a system with the following attributes:
- transparent;
- correct;
- complete;
- flexible;
- harmonized;
- clear;
- funded;
- encouraging long-term economic development.

Let us run briefly through these goals. A pension system theoretically can only be transparent if it is con- structed in such a way that there is a tight fit between contribution payments and entitlement to benefits. In this respect, the requirement for transparency is much more than a simple obligation to provide information, affecting as it does the essence of the system. Naturally, transparency involves a certain information-providing task, as the system has to be able to give all participants precise accounts.

Given the connection between contribution payments and benefit entitlements, it follows, almost as a matter of course – or at least as a rule of thumb – that the system must be defined contribution, rather than defined benefit. Because we support such a pension system, we believe the main task facing the current pension system is to extend the defined contribution subsystem, i.e. gradually transform the defined benefit subsystem.[34]

The pension system must be able to keep a precise tally of contribution payments. A clear relationship must be created between contribution payments and benefits provided, which spells out what one can expect to receive in return for what contributions; so the system has to be able to account for payments made by a participant to any "risk subsystem" – which means that contribution payments have to be formally divided between the risks.

Opponents of more transparent systems frequently object that a pension system should not be transparent, because that would kill solidarity. If people knew that a large part of their contribution payments was going to provide others (who have made little or no contribution themselves) with (higher) pension benefits (and it should be borne in mind that, for this latter group, this benefit fulfils an important social function), then they would demand an end to this redistribution, and those currently receiving benefits would cease to be provided for. Unfortunately, this is a lame argument! It supposes that people only "share goals" because they are ignorant. Those who espouse this point of view cannot conceive that people would consciously allow part of their contribution payments to serve purposes other than their own future wealth. We are much more optimistic on this question! In our interpretation, a transparent system allows the transparent redistribution (without direct remuneration) of contribution payments from one person to another, so in our opinion the level of solidarity can also – or rather *must* also – be made transparent. An additional advantage of this is that it allows consideration of whether the redistribution serves the proper purpose; whether it is going from the proper payer groups to the proper receiver groups, and in the proper measure; or whether redistribution is somehow failing. The issue would be resolved if only the opponents of open accounting admitted that today's system contains an element of "perverse redistribution", because the direction of redistribution is not so much from classes with higher income towards those with lower income, but exactly the opposite. In a more transparent system we are not left in the dark as regards "perverse redistribution": if such a problem arises, then it can be precisely measured, and it can be precisely defined where and to what extent the system has to be changed so that the unfavourable practice ends.

The goals and principles enumerated above are closely related to one another. As we have explained, exact accounting, i.e. correctness, is, in a sense, a preliminary and also a corollary of transparency. The shift to defined contributions is in itself a huge step toward correctness. But, at the same time, we should bear in mind that it is not just within the strictly defined pension system that unfairness arises between contribution payments and benefits received; it can also arise outside of it. And when a pension system is planned, this must be kept sight of and redressed.

In the case of a defined contribution system, unfairness should be examined in two places:

1. outside of the system, which means investigating whether the calculation of entitlements based on contribution payments is performed in a correct way;

2. within the system, where we must examine ways of switching from paying entitlements based on contribution payments to paying an annuity (and later changes in the level of the annuity).

The major source of unfairness outside of the system is neglecting the uneven distribution of the task of raising children and the division of labour within the family. It is often the case that, within the family, only one partner takes on a formal, full-time job, while the other partner either stays at home all of the time, or takes on a part-time job; or else (usually on account of having to raise children) is a formal wage earner for a shorter period of the active phase of the life cycle. As a result, formally only one partner (usually the man) receives a full pension entitlement on the basis of income that was, in reality, earned by both parties together; while the other partner (usually the woman) will receive only a partial entitlement. Certain distortions in the division of labour, though they involve independent "unfairness factors" in their own right, serve to reinforce this phenomenon: some jobs (such as doctors, teachers) have long been systematically underpaid, which means that people in those professions have a pension entitlement of an "incorrect" level. People who work in these fields often only take such a low-paying job because their spouse has a job that is paid better. Thus the phenomenon can, to some degree, be ascribed to the division of labour within the family. The problem might be solved by regrouping between the accounts of the couple. We will propose a method of achieving this.

A more complicated question is the unevenness of the burden of child-rearing *in society*. The fact is that raising children is of benefit to the whole of society – an "investment" in the future. But the burden of this investment is divided very unequally among the different members of society. Those who do not have children bear virtually none of the burden, while those who raise children bear more than an average load. One element of this greater-than-average burden is that, during the time they – usually the mothers – spend raising children, an adequate level of pension entitlement is not built up. Tackling this whole issue on the basis of correctness extends beyond the boundaries of the pension system, and so we will not deal with this question here; however, part of the solution could be forthe state to make additional contributions to the pension accounts of parents raising more children than average, with the money required for this coming from a tax on people with fewer than the average number of children (e.g. 0).[35] (We only suggest this as an idea, and do not pursue it in what follows.)

Another unfairness within the system might be if people's lifestyles are not reflected in their contributions and annuity. From this perspective, the utilization of a uniform, undifferentiated annuity table is certainly unfair. It is also unfair if we do not take account of changes that occur in mortality within the annuity tables (i.e. if we leave them unchanged for long periods).[36] Some important parameters that will certainly affect the life expectancy of different groups of the population are:

- gender;
- occupation (e.g. labourer or professional; affect would be even greater in the case of certain special occupations, such as miners);
- wealth and income status ("wealthy" and "poor");
- health status;
- bad habits (smoking, consuming alcohol, drugs, etc.).

The effect of some of these parameters on remaining life expectancy can easily be measured (e.g. gender), but others are more difficult to assess (e.g. wealth and income or health status, etc.). All in all, it would be correct if all parameters were taken into account when the starting level of the annuity was determined; but that can probably be achieved only gradually, over a period of time. As a first step, it would be enough to apply a table differentiated by gender (i.e. not the so-called "unisex" table).[37]

The problem of correctness also appears in the correct division of contribution loads between employee (insured), employer and the state. In our opinion, this is an illusory problem! The state is fundamentally not an independent income owner: it receives its income from employers and employees. Consequently, what the state gives to the system first has to be taken away from the other two players. It is clearer and simpler if it does not do this, and if only the primary characters take part in the cash flow (apart from the necessary co-ordinating role of the state).[38] The division of contribution payments between employee and employer is again a problem only in name. In reality, from the point of view of the employer, all expenditure benefits the employee, so it can be considered part of his wage. Whether in formal terms it is or is not is of secondary importance. Of course, it ceases to be an issue of secondary importance if the contribution elements of the employer and the employee fall under different taxation rules. But a tax system should not be handling money in different ways if it fulfils a similar function. We believe that a system in which the total pension contribution is part of the wage would be clearer, and so in what follows we describe such a system.

Finally we would like to point out an important technical consequence of implementing correctness. We might call this consequence partibility, meaning that a pension system built on this principle is in an equilibrium from a cross-sectional as well as a vertical sectional point of view, even in its smallest subsystem.

A limit to the correctness of a pension system is imposed by the need for some clearly defined level of solidarity, or a solidarity-based redistribution. The pension system has to be complete in the sense that it covers all needs connected to pension. So it has to provide a solution (at least a partial one) to poverty in old age, but should not encompass those who are certainly not threatened by this. Since the principles of solidarity and correctness are diametrically opposite, we suggest that the solidarity solutions be planted in a separate subsystem of the system. Accordingly, we suggest the establishment of a further pillar alongside (or in front of) the two existing compulsory pillars; logically we should call this "Pillar 0". Pillar I and Pillar II would become defined contribution systems in our model (or, more precisely, Pillar II would stay defined contribution), and Pillar 0 would function as a kind of old age support system.

An important problem in every support system is that it will attract free-riders. We must endeavour to keep this to a minimum under all circumstances, so the conditions for joining this support system must be stricter than for entering the normal system. This might be achieved by defining a relatively high age for entry (say to age 70, which could gradually be raised to 75, as the health of the population improves).

The form the support might take would be a national "basic pension", to which everyone over a certain entry age is entitled; but it could also be that an existing (or missing) pension is topped up to a defined level.

The source of the support might be the general tax income of the state, as well as a defined separate part of pension contributions.

It is important that the system should be able to adapt flexibly to changing needs, both at the individual and the organizational level. At the individual level, the system must be able to handle individuals entering and leaving the system, because in the future more and more people are expected to spend longer periods of time abroad – changing the countries, so to speak, in which they work during their life cycle. From their point of view, the pension system must be "portable": in other words, it must be flexible enough to follow their current workplace. Insured people will not work exclusively in full-time jobs, but will alternate between full-time, part-time and self-employment.

The system must also be able to handle the needs of employers arriving in (and later on possibly leaving) Hungary.

We believe that the pillar analogy will be suitable for describing the pension subsystems for some time to come. At the same time, we do not think that it is justified for individual pillars to operate according to different logic. This would cause a number of problems, and so we are in favour of a harmonized system. Important elements of harmonization are that every subsystem should be defined contribution; the individual accumulations should be recorded on individual accounts; and at retirement the starting level of annuity should be calculated following the same principles in every pillar, and later changes (increases) should also follow similar principles.

Another feature of harmonization is that the pension system must be harmonized with other elements of the social security system (e.g. healthcare system, provision for dependants, etc.). This is in keeping with the next goal.

We suggest that the pension system should be clear. Risks other than old age pension provision (and, in the method described later, the provision for widow/ers) should not be handled within its framework. Accordingly, we regard as pointless the controversy surrounding the question of developing disability pension and dependants' allowance in Pillar II. In our opinion, these elements should also be removed from Pillar I, and organized within a separate system. Naturally, this separate system will plug into the pension system at various points, but its goals and its logic are different, and the management of these risks does not belong within the old age pension system.

From the principle of correctness, it follows that a pension system must be totally funded, because only then is it certain that – at least at the level of a generation – all participants get back their own contribution payments, and that there are no systematic winner and systematic loser generations. Of course, being totally funded, this means that the current (unfunded) Pillar I (and later perhaps also Pillar 0, the other pillars already being funded) can only be modified over time. The current, unfunded situation has already created winners and losers, and the funding process itself will inevitably require some temporary sacrifices from certain generations – sacrifices that have to be made to ensure that it later functions correctly. Not all functioning modes of the pay-as-you-go system support funding. The fund account system that we propose makes Pillar I work by the same logic as Pillar II, thus creating the possibility of transfer between the two pillars and the gradual funding of Pillar I.[39]

Naturally, not only is funding important from the point of view of correctness, but it fundamentally enhances long-term economic development, the fulfilment of our last goal. This goal is especially important, since it is quite simply impossible to ignore the economic effects of such a system! Our proposed system promotes economic development largely through its funding tendency.

Funding means large-scale national capital accumulation, which forces the economy to be competitive. It makes Hungarian capital export possible, and thus, from an international perspective, it raises Hungarian citizens from their current position of economic subjugation to a position of proprietorship. Funding gradually decreases the pressure that pensions currently exert on the central government budget. Thus, it becomes easy (in the short term, or in the cross-section) to ensure that the annual budget is balanced, and the long-term (vertical sectional) balance of the system is automatically assured.

The Structure of the Pension System

Our proposed pension system would consist of the following elements:
1. support scheme for the elderly ("Pillar 0");
2. the pay-as-you-go scheme, based on individual accounts (Pillar I), which in the long term gradually becomes funded;
3. the funded scheme based on individual accounts (Pillar II);
4. other voluntary retirement savings (Pillar III).

The bulk of elements 3 and 4 in the above system are already functioning, and require only minor adjustments; but Pillar 0 has to be set up, and the existing Pillar I must be radically reformed. The state does not really have to deal with Pillar III; it is enough if the government offers general support for its operation and expansion.

In many respects, Pillar 0 fulfils a supplementary role, and its logic is very different from the functioning of the other pillars. In general, the other pillars operate as fund account schemes. The big question is: what should be credited to the accounts? In other words, who should pay, how much, in what system, and to whose account?

We believe that the currently valid model, in which new entrants onto the labour market are obliged to enter both Pillar I and Pillar II in a specified ratio, can be maintained in the long term. (The ratio of the two pillars can gradually change later on in favour of Pillar II.) But we propose extending the circle of insured to the following classes:

- self-employed people;
- homemaker spouses of employed and self-employed.

A pension contribution of a monthly fixed sum should be set for self-employed people, to be paid by them while they are working independently. The amount of the fixed contribution could be based on the value of the fund necessary for a minimally desirable pension level at that particular time, assuming an average career.

The same rules would apply to the spouses of employed and self-employed people, whether or not they are homemakers. These rules are:

- In case of divorce, the pension fund accumulated during marriage is treated as common property (unless stipulated otherwise in a marriage contract), which means that the arithmetical average of the funds accumulated during this period is taken,[40] and both parties receive this average (i.e. from the account of the party with the higher-than-average amount the difference is carried over to the account of the other party). If one or both parties are already retired, then the reserve of the commenced annuity is split according to these principles, and the two parties buy separate annuities. As for the premium reserve, the fund accumulated during marriage is decreased to the extent that the premium reserve has decreased since commencement of the annuity, as a result of the annuity payments.[41]
- If someone dies during the accumulation phase and leaves behind a widow/er, the widow/er inherits the accumulated fund, and it is carried over to his/her account (or if the widow/er is already retired, his/her premium reserve).
- If one half of the couple retires, but the other is not yet ready, then the annuity of the retiring person is calculated according to his/her

own pension capital – but in fact, as is described later, he/she will get not an annuity, but a planned withdrawal. When the other person also comes to retire, the premium reserve is then united with the already retired person's pension capital to buy a two-person annuity. The two-person annuity has the feature that, on first death of either partner, the annuity of the partner left cannot fall below 70% of the annuity received together (this parameter can be chosen freely between 70% and 100%).

- If a couple already in receipt of a two-person annuity divorce, then both parties receive their own entitlements earned before marriage, and the entitlements acquired during marriage have to be averaged; the premium reserve thus separated out will form the basis for the separate annuities.
- The entitlements of any insured person who dies during the accumulation phase without leaving a widow/er are inherited by the risk group; insured persons of the same age and gender inherit it in proportion to their accumulated fund.

The above rules would apply to Pillar I, since Pillar II has started operating using a somewhat different logic. That said, it would be useful to have the rules of the two pillars converge. For example, a rule could be introduced stipulating that the fund of a deceased person who was not single could only be inherited by the spouse, and that it could only be credited to the spouse's account (if the spouse doesn't have an account, one would be opened for him/her). As the rules that apply to the annuity phase have not yet even been worked out for Pillar II, they should be as for Pillar I in the first place.

It is important that unemployment and child-care benefit should be treated as wages, in the sense that they should attract pension contributions – that is, according to the general principles, the state would credit pension entitlements to the account of the insured, even during periods of unemployment and child-care (in both Pillar I and Pillar II).

In our opinion, it is useful if the pillars are not broken down into subsystems, but remain parts of one general system. Accordingly, we would be against having special rules that apply to certain professions (military, miners, etc.). But when the annuity is calculated, the time spent in those professions could be taken into account, if the profession in question is known to decrease the remaining life expectancy. In this case, the annuity could be calculated using a more favourable annuity table.

We do not recommend setting an age limit for retirement. The annuity level would depend on the age of the insured at retirement: for the same pot of money, the higher the age, the higher the starting level of the annuity can be. The system would thus provide an automatic incentive for people to retire later, and we could avoid the situation whereby the pensions of those retiring early are financed by others. To the minimum age of retirement the following rule could apply: an insured can retire only if, taking his/her age and accumulated fund into account, he/she can buy at least the minimum level of annuity. At the same time, this fund can be supplemented by top-up payments[42] at retirement and any time later on to increase the starting or the current level of the annuity. An annuity that has already commenced could be suspended any time (e.g. because someone "reactivates" himself), and in this case the premium reserve transforms again into a pension account, to which payments can be made.

One question is: what should happen to those who, even at a relatively advanced age, have not saved up a fund sufficient to buy the minimum level of annuity? For these insured, the annuity starts at the latest if they reach the age (we recommend 70–75 years) when the support system (Pillar 0) is triggered. Then the annuity purchased from their fund is topped up by Pillar 0 to the minimum level.

We recommend that the logic of Pillar I and Pillar II be as close to each other as possible. If this is realized, there is in theory no barrier to free movement between the two pillars. That said, this is not something we would recommend allowing: the pension system has to be funded over the long term, and so we only recommend allowing movement from Pillar I to Pillar II – and even this only in centrally commanded one-time steps (e.g. some years from now we would let the existing group of insured choose to divide their contribution between the two pillars in a ratio of 50:50, but for new employees this will be compulsory; still later, the ratio could move to 67:33 and so on).

A very positive advantage of defined contribution systems is that portability is relatively easily achieved. This is an important issue regarding the pension systems of different countries. If someone insured in Hungary subsequently wants to be insured in a different system – one that functions in basically the same way as the Hungarian – then it must be made possible for him to take his savings over to the other system (a transfer of "virtual" savings, but no less real for that). In the same way, someone from abroad who settles in Hungary could start his Hungarian "career" by paying his accumulated pension fund into the Hungarian system as a lump sum payment, dividing it between the two pillars according to the ratios that apply to new-entry employees. On the other hand, it should not be necessary for someone working abroad who joins a different pension system to be compelled to exit the Hungarian system. In principle, we see no obstacle to parallel membership (except that, for these insured, it is only possible to benefit from the support system based on the joint annuity – the foreign and home-grown annuities together).

Pillar 0: The Support System

When designing Pillar 0, we have to find a compromise between two contradictory principles: correctness and solidarity. One consequence of correctness is that everyone accumulates his savings for himself; this way everyone can see at once how their own savings are doing, and there is a direct stimulus to carry on with the contribution payments. The principle of solidarity dictates that society cannot wash its hands of those who have been unable, in the course of their active life, to accumulate a fund big enough for a minimum level of pension – irrespective of whether this is their own fault (e.g. because they "bilked" contribution payments and preferred to spend the money during their active life) or not (because they didn't have the ability or the chance to work in a job with a salary high enough for a long enough period of time). On the other hand, the higher the level of pension received on the basis of solidarity, the weaker the incentive for the insured to pay contributions into the pension system and the stronger the free-rider strategy. Accordingly, participation in Pillar 0 should be made quite difficult, so that the incentive to pay contributions into Pillars I and II is not significantly decreased.

We envisage making participation in Pillar 0 difficult by setting the age limit for entitlement to a pension from Pillar 0 significantly higher than the usual retirement age. This age limit should be around the age when – taking the average physical and mental state of the given society – people generally are not able to earn enough by work to cover their current consumption. In Hungary, we expect the health of the population to improve gradually in the future, and so the age limit can gradually be raised (perhaps have the rise built in – say an increase of one month every year). We suggest setting the age limit at 70 when the system is started.

The benefit received could be of two types:

1. a basic citizen's pension that everyone receives;
2. a top-up to whatever pension is received from Pillars I and II.

We propose choosing type two, since it obviously costs less than type one. The cost of the support benefit is an important aspect: it is need that governs solidarity expenditure, and the bulk of the population – hopefully – will not be in need of the basic citizen's pension.

A top-up would be provided automatically if the pension received from Pillars I and II fails to reach the minimum level, or if the citizen receives no benefits from either pillar. This does somewhat conflict with the principle of being in need, since it is possible that the individual has plenty of income from private savings, letting an apartment, etc.; however, we are of the opinion that it is not worth maintaining a separate apparatus to examine the true state of neediness, because this is very difficult to reckon in most cases.

Regarding the minimum level of pension, we suggest defining two types:
1. subsistence level;
2. social minimum.

The subsistence level would always be defined and kept up to date by means of a pensioners' "consumption basket". This would be the minimum level to which Pillar 0 would complement the annuity of Pillars I and II after the age of 70 (possibly until the annuity from these two pillars exceeds this level). The social minimum would be higher than the subsistence level. This would be tied to an average, normal consumption level for society, based on consumption among the active population. This minimum level would be used to determine when the insured is entitled to ask for benefit payments from Pillar I and Pillar II.[43] Below the age of 70, a person would be allowed to retire if – taking account of his current age – the fund accumulated in Pillar I and Pillar II was enough to purchase an annuity of at least the level of the current social minimum.

Pillar I: The Fund Account System

According to our previous discussion, the pay-as-you-go system is not an alternative to the funded system. The pay-as-you-go system is also funded, with the special features that:
1. what covers the total pension capital is state debt; and
2. this is not explicitly demonstrated.[44]

The implicit nature of the capital generates the illusion among most observers that this capital does not even exist.[45] Transforming Pillar I into a fund account system changes the second feature, making the debt explicit – moreover, broken down to the level of the individual. This way the term "notional" in the original name of this system is misleading, and may be interpreted as a kind of concession to the common view: since, according to the commonly held view, a defined contribution system is explicitly funded under all circumstances, the not-explicitly-funded system can only be a "virtual", "notionally" defined contribution (in other words "fund account") system. Thus we propose to call the new system simply a fund account system, rather than experimenting with the "virtual fund account" terminology, since the term "notional" or "virtual" induces almost every opponent of the system to make fun of these terms and verbally discredit the system, and even misleads advocates of the system by suggesting that this is not a "real fund account".[46]

The fund account system is usually regarded as a pay-as-you-go system, and it is indeed a system of this kind (with the proviso shortly to be stated) in the sense that its reserves are exclusively in state debt, not formally printed (and not recorded in the state balance sheet – at least not at present – as state debt, although it is made explicit and registered through the fund accounts). On the other hand, the fund account system satisfies the criterion of individual equivalence, i.e. the vertical sectional equivalence, and thus it only rarely satisfies the criterion of cross-sectional equivalence, and consequently cannot be a "pure" pay-as-you-go system in the "classical" sense.[47]

The level of currently payable contributions can never be based on the currently payable annuities – only on the annuities to be paid in the future. So either the central budget has to be prepared to cover the deficit (or a wage tax-like[48] element handling temporary deficits has to be built into the system) or it must be able to handle the reserves built up from temporary surpluses.

The fund account system offers the possibility of providing a maximally correct pension for everyone from the pay-as-you-go system. But it does not automatically make the system financially viable. In a sense, contribution income and benefit payments depend on separate demographic processes, so there is no guarantee of their being balanced. In order for the state to be prepared well in advance for periods when, for demographic reasons, income systematically fails to cover expenditure, it is prudent to create long-term reserves – what we might call "demographic" reserves. The fund account system can only function well if complemented by such funded elements.

As a first step, then, we try to review the cash flow of the fund account system, with special respect to this long-term reserve.

Cash Flow in the Fund Account System

The following figure introduces schematically the possible cash flows of the fund account system. Later on we shall build a simple model based on this, and try to give some kind of estimate of the necessary level of reserves according to this model. We use the following notation in the figure:

$H(t)$ explicit state debt at the t point in time
h the interest rate of the state debt
$A(t)$ the level of the demographic reserve
a the interest rate of the demographic reserve
$V(t)$ the balance of the fund accounts
i the interest rate of the fund accounts
$J(t)$ income from contribution payments
$E(t)$ other ("demographic") payments into the demographic reserve
$N(t)$ pension annuity payments
Implicit state debt at the t point in time = $V(t) - A(t)$

Figure 4. The cash flows of the fund account system

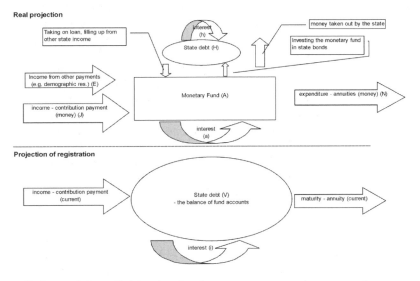

It is useful to divide the fund account system into two planes: a "real" and a "registration" plane (projection). These two are connected through the current income (contribution payments) and expenditure (annuities), which are the same values in both planes at every point in time. As we have already indicated, we imagine the fund account system as a "pure" system, which means that it includes no element of the current Pillar I, apart from the old age pension.

The individual accounts are administrated on the registration plane. All current contribution payments are credited to the accounts, and pension benefit payments decrease the balance of the accounts.[49] There is mainly implicit state debt behind the balance of the fund accounts, so the benefit payments can be regarded as the maturity of part of the state debt. But the fund accounts are not covered exclusively by (implicit) state debt, but also by the Monetary Fund indicated on the figure, which we might as well call "demographic reserve". Subtracting the value of the demographic reserve from the current balance of the fund accounts, we get the implicit state debt (that is behind the fund account system – not generally![50]).

In the real projection we examine the actual cash flow and reserving, and the explicit debt. Formally (since, in reality, the system will probably be much more complicated), we look at it as all contribution payments flowing into the Monetary Fund (the demographic reserve), and all expenditures (annuity benefits) being covered from this fund. If the current contribution payment exceeds current expenditure, the difference is reserved and invested. It is important that only investment outside of the state system can be considered as investment, so the purchase of government bonds is not investment.[51] If the Monetary Fund contains assets, and the current contribution payments do not cover current annuities, then part of the assets in the Monetary Fund are used to cover the deficit. If the money in the fund is not sufficient for this, then the state compensates for this from other sources, e.g. by increasing the (explicit) state debt. If the assets of the Monetary Fund are invested in state bonds after all, then this is expediently viewed as the value of the fund decreasing, and the value of the explicit state debt increasing.[53] Repaying the explicit state debt is the business of the state, and has nothing to do with the fund account system later on (and there is no need to keep a record of whether the explicit state debt was created due to the payment of pensions or some other reason).[54]

The state can also take away the money generated in the Monetary Fund (this is what usually happens!), e.g. to cover other current expenses of the social welfare system. In this case, the value of the Monetary Fund drops, and the implicit state debt grows by the same amount.

The Monetary Fund can have other systematic income sources, besides contributions and the occasional top-up (or continuous) payments made by the state. The term "other" refers to contributions that generate no entitlements; as these payments are not registered later on the individual fund accounts, they may be viewed as a kind of tax. The most important such systematic income consists of payments made for demographic equalization, which is primarily what is discussed here.

We call the demographic reserve "demographic", because it is needed to handle demographic fluctuations, which are capable of causing a significant difference between current income and current expenditure. Fortunately, the fund account system can be launched in such a way that, at the outset and for a fairly long time afterwards, the income from current contribution payments exceeds current expenditure. But given the Hungarian demographic tendencies, it is clear that current expenditure will gradually come to exceed current income, and will continue to do so for a long time. This situation may be regarded as repayment of part of the implicit state debt that has fallen due. A truly heedful state does not make these repayments from its current "other" income ("other" meaning not involving the pension system), but creates reserves in advance to cover them. This is what we call a demographic reserve, and its source may be regular state income for this purpose (such as a "wage tax"), or simply the regrouping and accumulation of certain state incomes.

The Content of the Fund Account, Movements on the Account and the Movements of the Account

The life of an account has two clearly distinct phases: the accumulation phase and the annuity payout phase. At first, there is a strict separation between these; but later on the phases may alternate (suspending and restarting payment of the annuity), and even overlap (when the annuitant performs a top-up payment to the account in order to increase the level of the annuity received).[55] Because of all these, it is important that the account is registered even in the annuity phase, until the end of the insured's life. Moreover, since inheriting the account is also possible, keeping track of such accounts may even become necessary in the case of those not yet in the active phase of life (virtually from birth). With the above proviso, we shall examine separately the registration of the accumulation and the annuity phases of the account.

Let us start with the accumulation account, and with the questions that arise here (in the certain knowledge that even the "simple" questions – how interest accrues and how to credit the account – are quite complicated).

"Complicated" problems include handling inheritance, death during the active phase, the relationship with disability and dependants' benefits, unique account movements (subtractions, transfers) and possible unification of accounts (at the end of the accumulation phase, to receive two-person annuities). These problems need to be discussed and, if possible, consensus should be reached. Here we give only a few recommendations.

In the case of death during the active phase, we see the following possibilities for handling the account:[56]

1. Living members of the risk community could inherit this account value, and have it divided up among them risk-proportionately (initially, this means considering the age and the account balance of each insured; later on it would include other factors, too). This method decreases the level of contributions necessary.

2. It could be inherited freely: that is – just as with private pension funds – the insured could declare a beneficiary (or beneficiaries). Inheritance could only take the form of a credit to the individual account balance. In the case of underage beneficiaries, an account would immediately be opened; in the case of active beneficiaries, the sum would simply be added to the account value; and in the case of annuitants, the level of the annuity would be raised at the same time as the sum is credited to the account (to the same extent as the fund is increased by the credited sum). If the insured does not declare a beneficiary, the account balance is added to the account of the next of kin; if there is no next of kin, the pension capital would be divided according to either solution 1 or solution 4.

3. To help neutralize demographic fluctuations, the account balance of the deceased could be formally changed to state bonds, which could be used to create balance in the system (cross-sectional balance). This method reduces the need for wage tax-like contributions. The formal exchange is necessary so that the state does not have the chance to "deny" this kind of contribution to the system.

4. It could replace part of the dependants' subsystem – the widow/er's provision (including common-law marriages), with the sum being credited to the fund account of the widow/er. The account balance of an insured person who dies without leaving a widow/er would be inherited by the risk community.

We consider all of the above methods possible, though it should be borne in mind that the issues discussed later depend on the method chosen at this point. We have a preference for method 4 (although a plus point in favour of method 1 is that generally we prefer pure subsystems, which means that we also suggest organizing the provisions for orphans in a pure subsystem in Pillar I). There are a number of arguments in favour of method 4:

1. The pension can be regarded basically as a family venture. The current widow/er's provision (which incidentally reflects the logic of a different age) would be rendered meaningless, as the old age pension system would take over its purpose.

2. It is not easy to justify free inheritance, because the account balance and the needs of the dependants have nothing to do with one another. Moreover, it is difficult to construct the fund account so that it can allow for other needs besides old age pension and widow/er's benefits. It would not be expedient to solve the inheritance with immediate cash payment, since this step is theoretically alien to a system based on implicit state debt. This way the account balance as a legacy could only be credited to another fund account, but then the question again rises – what function has this in the system?

3. The division of the capital of those dying without leaving a widow/er (or dying as a widow/er) among the living members of the risk community is in harmony with the "philosophy of the system", since we suppose age-group risk communities, so the living members of the risk community have to inherit!

It is also useful to set up accounts for the dependants' benefits – narrowed down to the orphan's benefit, one per dependant. This account would be separate from the fund account of the dependant (if indeed the dependant has such an account). The sum credited to the account would be the expected present value of the dependant's benefits, and its balance value would fall as benefits are paid out. The source of this present value would primarily be the contribution payments flowing into the subsystem of dependants' provisions, or – in the case of solution 3 (which we do not suggest, by the way) – partly the individual account of the testator.

In case of disability, the individual account would remain in the accumulation phase, but the source of contribution payments arriving in this account would be the disability subsystem. The contributions paid to the account would be part of the disability benefit (up to an official age limit).[57] Once the age limit is reached, the disability pension is terminated, and payment of the old age pension is started from the account, according to the general rules.[58] In the case of death below the age limit, the procedure again follows the general rules.

If the disabled person recovers, and the disability pension is terminated, then the fund account will function according to the general rules in every respect.

The account has to be able to handle individual account movements: that is, occasional top-up payments (made by the insured) and supports (received from the employer, a wealthy uncle, etc.); other regular money transfers (e.g. by a spouse based on a marriage contract); backdated missed contribution payments recovered from an employer, plus interest; and deductions (e.g. in case of divorce or during child rearing).[59]

In a sense, the regular subdivision among the living members of the risk community of the account values of those dying without leaving a widow/er can also be regarded as a unique account movement (though in a different sense it is absolutely regular). Here we have to define precisely who would inherit the account value of the deceased and the ratio in which it would be subdivided. We also have to take into account that the insured persons of a given age group could – if they so wished – be in the accumulation phase, as well as in the annuity phase of the account (moreover they could toggle between these phases). Thus we have to make a decision on two points:

1. We have to decide whether those insured who belong to both the accumulation and the annuity phase belong to the same or to a different risk community.
2. We have to decide whether we define risk communities by age group, or whether all age groups belong to the same risk community.

Our proposal is that the accumulation and the annuity phases should be separated, and within these only those with the same birth year should form a risk community. So if, for example, the owner of an account in the accumulation phase dies, then the balance value would be subdivided among the owners of accumulating accounts born in the same year, in proportion to their account balance.[60] We do not suggest barring spouses from "inheriting" from the risk community, since in theory they could also at any time leave the balance of their accounts to the risk community.

Naturally, the annuity and the accumulation phases can alternate several times; thus it is possible that someone belongs to one risk group at the beginning of the year, to the other at the end of the year, and once again to the first risk group at the beginning of the next year. The reserve of the suspended annuity transforms into an accumulating account, from which the owner will receive an annuity later on, according to the currently effective annuity table, rather than the one used previously.

Since, for married couples, we suggest the purchase of two-person annuities, this requires that, at the beginning of the annuity phase, and also later on, the accounts can be united – or separated (in case of divorce). This also means that, in the annuity phase, two-person accounts are possible. (We exclude this possibility in the accumulation phase, due to the complicated handling of divorces, etc. Instead of the two-person accounts, we suggest regrouping on certain occasions.)

From what has been said, it is clear that a well-thought-out fund account system cannot go without running the accounts in the annuity phase. The content of the accounts depends on the extent to which the benefit is given or can be chosen freely in the annuity phase, but this will be discussed in more detail later on.

We suggest managing the money of the insured on the account, in both the accumulation and the annuity phase, in units – just as with investment funds and unit-linked life insurances. This greatly simplifies the task of determining how much the payments made at different times have contributed to the current balance of the account, since it is only necessary to look up the number of units bought by a given payment, and the present value of these units is exactly the current value of the units. Thanks to the unit-based administration, indexation of both the fund account and the annuity can be performed quite simply. One consequence of this technique is that the days of spectacular rises in pensions are left behind, as are unnecessary and pointless disputes related to these, since, using this technique, pensions rise gradually – month by month – as the unit values increase.

The value of units increases continuously (each day), such that the annual level achieved is the gross wage index of the previous year. (One could say that this will be the promised yield of the implicit state debt.) If this is a negative value, then the value of units decreases, too.

The natural way in which a fund account is terminated is following the death of the insured. But it may be necessary to build other modes of termination into the system, too. This is because of international labour force migration, possibly involving change of citizenship. Of course, this is bi-directional migration: employees and insured not only leave Hungary, but also arrive in the country. This is not necessarily important from the perspective of the pension system, since it may well be imagined that someone who leaves Hungary will still remain a member of the Hungarian pension system, and will even receive a pension from it later on (parallel to pensions received from other systems). Leaving the Hungarian pension system should not be obligatory. In the same way, if someone arrives in Hungary, he can become a member of the Hungarian pension system and at the same time keep his membership of his former system, so no accounting need take place between the two systems.

On the other hand, there are several cases when accounting between two systems and transfer from one system to the other might be necessary. The most important such cases are:

1. change of citizenship, and the associated requirement to be part of only one pension system;
2. the pension received from one or both systems being too low, so that it becomes necessary to unify entitlements.

The first case can be handled by accounting between different pension systems, provided there is an agreement on this between the Hungarian and the other pension system. Within this framework, the sum of the fund account (and the account in Pillar II) of the emigrant is transferred to the pension system of the receiving country, and there it will become a component of the individual's pension entitlements. The capital of immigrants is transferred to the Hungarian system from the former system, and it will generate Hungarian pension entitlements for the immigrant, according to the general regulations. If there is no agreement in existence between the systems, then the capital of those individuals leaving Hungary must be given to them in cash; those arriving in Hungary can decide whether or not to pay the capital they have received from the old system into the Hungarian pension system (contribution payments are only compulsory on income earned in Hungary).

The second case can only be handled if an agreement exists between the Hungarian and the other pension system. In this case it is handled in a way similar to that described in case one.

Problems Related to Contribution Payments

There are many problems that arise in connection with contribution payments. Those that we consider the most important are as follows.

What attracts interest: the prescribed contribution or the contribution actually paid?
On this point, we would like to state a principle: the principle of contribution drive or, in other words, precise accounting. According to this principle, only contributions actually paid in can bear interest. Of course, if payment of the contributions does not depend on the employee, yet he is the one to bear the negative consequences of late payments, then he must be protected against the possible negligence of the employer. Thus, an employee can sue his employer for missed contribution payments plus interest (naturally the sum gained goes to the fund account).

Should there be an age limit and/or a minimum payment period?
As we outlined earlier, we do not want to define liability for contribution payments by a period of time or by age, but by how much capital has been accumulated.

Is there a maximum level of contribution payment?[60]
We do suggest an upper limit on contributions. Above this limit, the capital can be withdrawn in a lump sum; below the limit – and up to it – the capital can be topped up. At the same time, we consider it a priority for the individual to collect the amount required for the necessary level of pension *as early as possible*; so the good years, which may never return, should be exploited to the full in this respect. Thus there should be no upper limit on contributions, but only on the accumulated capital that can be converted into an annuity. Moreover, if the income is high, then paying contributions is a much smaller problem. Thus we suggest that it should be compulsory to pay contributions as a percentage of total income, until such time as the balance of the fund account reaches the level at which the insured's pension would be at the social minimum level if he retired at that moment. Above this, all contribution payment would be voluntary, and could even be abandoned totally.

Is it possible to make occasional top-up contribution payments or to receive the capital value of the annuity as a lump sum payment?
Certainly – up to the upper limit mentioned previously.

What should the level of the contribution be?
As will be discussed later, in calculating the annuity, we propose an interest rate of 0% and (as we said earlier) wage index-based indexation (in both the accumulation and the annuity phases). Based on this, we get a simple formula for the necessary level of contribution, then we

get the following simple formula for the contribution,[61] assuming an individual who works all his life and always earns the average wage:

$$j = \frac{h \cdot e}{ra - k} \text{ where}$$

j: the necessary contribution level
h: the targeted gross substitution rate (i.e. substitution measured in the gross,[62] rather than the net wage)
ra: the targeted retirement age (mainly for calculation, rather than compulsion!)
k: average age of starting career
e: remaining life expectancy, effective at the official retire ment age

If we substitute the following values into this formula:

h = 50%, e = 16.25, ra = 62, k = 22, then the necessary level of contribution has the following value:

So the starting contribution level of the system should be approximately 20%, given the parameters currently effective.[63] The formula gives an upper estimate under all circumstances, since it does not take account of the effect of inheriting the account of deceased insured.

Who pays the contribution?
We believe it would be better if this contribution came from one source (the employee) instead of two sources (the employer and the employee), though in such a way that it would still be declared and paid by the employer. According to this design, the wage would have the following structure:

Net wage + personal income tax = "small gross" wage. The base of personal income tax is the "small gross" wage.
Gross wage = "small gross" wage + contributions (pension and other) The gross wage would be the base of the possible wage tax.

How is the annual balance of the system reached?
As we saw above, the fund account system does not automatically fulfil the criterion of cross-sectional equilibrium. There are two solutions to this:
  1. the state assumes the liability of covering the deficiency in every year;

2. the excesses are reserved in the system, and shortfalls are covered by a wage tax, proportional to the gross wage paid by the employer – a so-called "demographic wage tax".

We prefer solution 2. It is important to stress that it is unwise to force contributions to a level that would provide cross-sectional balance, and this is why we think it important to cover shortfalls through a different type of payment (a wage tax).

The necessary level of contribution can be varied as the parameters of the above formula change (primarily the life expectancy projection, secondly the age limit, etc.), and that has to be "communicated" to the insured.

Pillar II and Other Pillars: Individual Funding

In what has gone before, we imagined Pillar I being reformed along the lines of Pillar II. This was for a very good reason: in the model we propose, the two pillars function in a totally analogous way, and – in a sense – become totally permeable. But this also requires certain changes to Pillar II. The most important areas that need to be changed in the current Pillar II are:
1. the accounting, reviewing technique;
2. the rules of inheritance;
3. the benefit payment.

The technique of accounting should be similar both in the private pension funds (not just the private pension funds belonging to Pillar II, but also the voluntary pension funds) and in our proposed system of Pillar I; following the example of investment funds, the sum in the accounts of members should be registered in units here as well. One might also say that the accumulating account of the private fund as a "product" should converge with the investment fund as a product.[64]

It is also important that the current rules governing inheritance should be changed. Currently, the owner of the account declares an heir. But this must be changed, so that, come what may, it is the *spouse* of the owner of the account – if there is one – who inherits the account. The mode of inheritance would, in this case, involve transfer of the balance value to the private fund account of the spouse. We do not believe that changing the rules of inheritance in this way would cause too much upset, since presumably even now it is usually the spouse who inherits.

Far greater opposition might be expected from another aspect of the planned move to bring Pillar I and Pillar II into line with one another: if it is no longer possible under Pillar II for anybody but the spouse to inherit, then anyone who dies without leaving a living spouse would have his account inherited by the living members of the risk community. Although this step would be necessary for complete harmonization, the harmony of the two systems could be achieved at a satisfactory level without this measure.

It would be important to introduce similar rules for divorce as are proposed for Pillar I, where the two accounts are put together and divided equally between the two parties – unless a marriage contract stipulates otherwise.

Finally, the received benefit, the annuity, would have to be defined in a way something like the mode defined in the following section. Regarding the benefit, in Pillar II there is also the question of who will provide it. Under our proposals, only life insurance companies or annuity insurers specially founded for this purpose are allowed to provide these benefits – mainly because well-thought-out rules of guarantee already apply to these institutions, and it would be unnecessary for new types of institutions to be created if existing ones can adequately fulfil the function. The annuity provided under Pillar II would be special, in that it would have to be able to handle the merging of single-person annuities into two-person annuities, and also the division of two-person annuities into single-person annuities, etc. Since these refer to annuities received from different providers, the individual providers will have to be able to transfer between them the reserve of annuities that have already started (which is not customary in the case of annuities currently provided by life insurers). We suggest giving the insured the right to change provider during the term – whether or not divorce, etc. is involved – and to transfer their annuity reserve to another provider (e.g. because the other provider usually achieves higher yields than the current one). The major parameters of the annuity (accounting performed in units, 0% interest rate, differentiation by gender) would be the same in Pillar II as is proposed for Pillar I.

In case of voluntary pension funds, we do not propose any changes to the current system, apart from unit-based accounting. Here there is no need to change the rules of inheritance, and we do not suggest regulating the annuity in the same way as in Pillar I. The only new rule that we propose regarding the annuity is that voluntary pension funds would only be allowed to provide a financial ("certain") annuity; they would not be allowed to provide life annuities, which require an adequate risk community and sufficient solvency capital, as these requirements would be passed on to life insurance companies.

With the introduction of the above rules, Pillar I and Pillar II become practically transferable. (One could also say that, as a consequence of the above, Pillar I practically becomes a gigantic private pension fund.) But why is this necessary? Currently – apart from the various short-term campaigns to get people to switch – there is only one kind of transfer allowed between the two pillars: in case of disability, the amount accumulated in Pillar II is transferred to Pillar I, and this will provide the disability benefit. This method is problematic in many respects,[65] but it is not necessary in the system we propose, as we suggest organizing disability benefit in a separate subsystem that is independent of both Pillar I and Pillar II. So the question arises: what kind of transfers should we allow between the two pillars? This will be discussed more in relation to the possible further development of the system, but we would like to say in advance that we primarily suggest a gradual, long-term, guided transfer from Pillar I to Pillar II.

Regarding Pillar II, the present situation is that a special institutional arrangement is being put in place around a precisely defined product. But the nature of the product is such that it could equally well be operated by other institutions (mainly life insurance companies and investment providers), so there is no need to limit the potential institutional diversity (or only in the accumulation phase). Instead of the institution, we should focus on the product.

The Benefit: The Annuity

We imagine that the annuity would look something like those market-based annuities currently available, employing the basic principles embedded in their structure. This is what satisfies the criterion of actuarial correctness. But this does not mean that we suggest using exactly the same annuities as are on offer on the market at present. It does mean, though, that some direct competition might build up between the annuities of Pillar I and Pillar III.

Since the annuity of Pillar I is practically compulsory for everyone, the annuities used here can have the kind of flexible features that would be problematic in Pillar III – essentially this means features like being able to change the benefits provided after the annuity has started; being able to unite single-person annuities; and being able to divide two-person annuities. But once the annuities of Pillar I have such features, they are more likely to be introduced in the other pillars.

The annuity that Pillar II will provide is currently not regulated. We suggest that it should follow the annuity of Pillar I, as described here, in every respect (apart from the level of indexation).

We have already explained several features of the annuity, and here we try to summarize these features in an organized way. First we talk about a few important and very general features:

- The annuity (like accumulating fund accounts) would be defined in units (which is a solution similar to the points system). The reserve of the annuity would also be determined in units. In the annuity phase, the number of units that are regularly paid can change for only one reason: the mortality profit (loss) is credited to the account. Apart from this, and apart from such changes as making top-up payments, suspending the annuity, uniting single-person annuities or dividing two-person annuities, the number of units regularly being paid remains unchanged from the time the annuity commences to the date it is terminated by death (assuming the technical interest rate to be 0%).

- We suggest setting the technical interest rate at 0% (please define!). The reason for this is that it is particularly important to maintain the value of the annuity, and we prefer to see a faster increase during the term to a higher exchange rate on commencement of the annuity, since we think this is safer. The 0% would be a uniform rate: that is, the insured does not have the option of choosing a higher technical interest rate, and thereby selecting a higher starting level for the annuity, which would then always increase at a lower rate. In Pillar II, no provider would be allowed to deviate from this interest rate. The 0% also fits the rule that – apart from the obvious exceptions – the number of units of the annuity (namely the units that are regularly being paid) is unchanged. If a higher technical interest rate were chosen, the number of units would have to be proportionately decreased yearly.

- We suggest that there should be no guarantee period (either at the beginning or at the end of the annuity). We do not want to apply this remnant of widow/er's and orphan's benefits, since we propose handling these issues in a more mature way. (This also means that we suggest not letting this element appear in Pillar II.)

- We propose the gross wage index[66] as the indexation level. This way, the pensions will more or less follow average wages, which is a requirement of pension systems that is often emphasized and acknowledged. Indexation simply means regularly increasing the value of units, so that the annuity increases. The value of units can grow continuously (which is what we propose), but it could also be increased once a year. This is something to be decided.

The following annuity types can occur as benefits, but the insured has no option to choose – it is clearly defined what must be applied in which situation:

1. single-person annuity for those entering the pensioner age as singles and for those divorcing during the annuity phase;
2. regular, annuity-like withdrawal from the fund account for a married person[67] whose spouse remains active at the time of retirement;
3. two-person annuity for retired couples.

The need to differentiate by gender follows from the criterion of actuarial correctness. However, this criterion governs not only differentiation by gender, but also by every factor that can be known (e.g. health, bad habits, education, residence); this deeper differentiation can only be achieved gradually, over a longer period of time. The reason for this is that there are not many tangible objective factors, apart from gender, for which the effect on remaining life expectancy is known; for example, residence can change regularly, and even education is not such a permanent factor as gender. And there is currently no mechanism for performing an objective survey of health without there being a significant risk of fraud. So further differentiation is a programme for the longer term, and one that can be gradually realized through the extensive analysis of mortality factors and the development of a system that enables adequate objective study. While we are on the subject of differentiation, we should point out that differentiation by health rewards bad habits, for example alcoholism and smoking, which place an additional burden on the health service. So it is correct to take these factors into consideration only if they are also calculated for contributions to the health service.

The regular withdrawal of money can be regarded as a financial (certain) annuity for an indefinite period if the insured already receives benefits but is not yet a member of any wider risk community. Withdrawal of money can occur in only one scenario – in a marriage, when one partner already receives a pension, but the other partner would like to remain active. If the marriage ends in the meantime (either by divorce or on the death of the active partner), then regular withdrawal from the account ceases, and the existing reserve must be converted into a single-person annuity (in the event of the death of the active partner, the fund balance value of the active partner is added to the starting capital of the annuity). If the insured dies during the period of withdrawal, then the active spouse inherits the pension capital. Actually, keeping open the possibility of this inheritance is the reason that a spouse cannot receive a single-person annuity even temporarily, because, in the case of a single-person annuity, it is the risk community that inherits the premium reserve of the deceased, and not the widow/er.

The withdrawal of money depletes the capital on the account faster than if it were changed to an annuity. The reason for this is that, with an annuity, not only does the premium reserve of the annuitant decrease with the annuity payments, but it also increases with that part of the disengaged capital of deceased members of the risk community that is credited to each living member. This element of increase is missing if the money is withdrawn regularly; thus the amount withdrawn cannot reach the level that the insured would receive as annuity benefit if the pension capital were changed to a single-person annuity. The size of withdrawal that can be allowed depends partly on unknown factors,[68] so we suggest applying a simple rule when the system is launched. According to this rule, the amount to be withdrawn must be at least the social minimum, but cannot be more than two-thirds of the single-person annuity that the insured would receive, taking account of his current age, when withdrawal commences. This also means that an insured person with a spouse still active cannot retire (although he can stop being active) until sufficient capital has been accumulated to allow the withdrawal of money.[69]

A two-person annuity can be started if the benefit received is at least twice the social minimum. Concerning this limit, the insured couple can choose between two types of two-person annuity:

1. where the benefit received falls to two-thirds of the original value after the death of the first insured;
2. where the benefit received remains the same after the death of the first insured.

It is clear that the second type of annuity is more expensive, but its benefit is not necessarily required.

All three types of benefit (single-person annuity, withdrawal of money, two-person annuity) can be suspended for an indefinite period, should the insured so wish. During this period, the fund account is changed to an accumulating account and its capital earns interest. The insured may also wish to make further contribution payments up to a certain prescribed limit, but there is no longer any requirement to do so. They can restart benefit payments at any time, with the proviso that the type of benefit (single-person annuity, two-person annuity, money withdrawal) will depend on the current family circumstances and the activity of the spouse. Naturally, at a later stage, the calculated annuity should be higher than before the annuity was suspended (that is the incentive to suspend). During suspension, the capital is inherited according to the rules governing an accumulating account in the event of death of the insured.

If two annuitants marry, their premium reserves are added together and a two-person annuity must be calculated, based on the combined capital value. If two annuitants divorce, the premium reserve is divided between them in the ratio 50:50, and they both have to buy a single-person annuity from their share. If an annuitant marries a person who is still active, then the annuity is stopped and a regular withdrawal of money commences, according to the general rules.

The insured can, at any time and up to a certain limit, make top-up payments into the system. This does not change the amount of money withdrawn, but the level of annuities already commenced is raised, as if the top-up payment has been used to purchase a new annuity.

There is an understandable desire on the part of the insured to gain some idea, even in the accumulation phase, of the level of annuity that will be received on retirement. A great advantage of defined benefit systems is that this question can be answered relatively easily. Many think that defined contribution systems cannot answer this question at all. Fortunately this is not so, although they can only give conditional answers. The conditional answer runs something like this: "If you retire at age x, and the current annuity table is still effective, and if you continue to build your pension capital at the current rate, then the starting level of a single-person annuity will be y units, which, at the current exchange rate, works out at z Hungarian forints." We suggest that the social security system should provide this type of information annually to every insured, for at least three values of x (e.g. 60, 65, and 70 years). In the same way, it should state for every x value what the level of the annuity would be, using the current annuity table, for the number of units built up so far.

We would like to keep the defined contribution character, even after the annuity has commenced. This means that we suggest applying the effects of changes in mortality and remaining life expectancy to the benefits.. This would have the effect that, at any given moment, we use only one mortality table, whether we are calculating an annuity that is commencing, or the reserve of one already started. When checking the mortality table, the mortality profit or loss is accounted in commenced annuities by changing the number of units. It is useful to avoid great changes in the benefits paid when these corrections are performed,[70] so the mortality table always has to be set very carefully.

It is important that the annuity must always be calculated based on a projected population mortality, rather than current mortality. This is because, in developed countries, mortality has decreased over the past decades, and life expectancy has significantly increased. It is expected that this effect will reach Hungary as well. A mortality table that reflects the past does not give an adequate calculation background for annuities. This is what makes projection necessary, and of course it has to be refreshed constantly and kept up to date. Refreshing the table has several effects:

1. It changes the expected annuity. If the annuity is significantly decreased, then perhaps the contribution level or the retirement age suggested by the state as the norm has to be increased, so that the pension level that the state finds desirable can be achieved by pensioners later on.

2. It changes the current annuity and premium reserve of the annuitants.

3. It changes the amount of monetary instruments necessary to maintain the cross-sectional balance, and thus influences the level of wage tax.

The changes resulting from the changes in the projection (primarily the change in the expected pension for those still active, and the expected change in wage tax and contributions) have to be communicated in a proper form to those affected. (The proper form is: letter, home page, TV, information programmes in various media, etc.) They must also be told when to expect the changes (when a new projection is made).

The system can only function well if ever more precise projections are made of the population changes – mainly the remaining life expectancies – and if these are regularly maintained. It would be useful if an independent demographic research centre could be set up (e.g. under the supervision of parliament) with a precisely defined task and access to all the necessary data on the pension system. The pension institute would be expected to make good use of the projections, i.e. it would be expected to change the annuity tables and the annuity reserves. To make the changes foreseeable, the projections would have to be refreshed at regular intervals – say every 3–5 years.

As we have already mentioned, we suggest introducing the above benefit structure not only in Pillar I, but also in Pillar II. In the case of Pillar I, the provider is clearly the social security system, controlled by the state – as is the manager of the fund accounts. But in the case of Pillar II, this is not so obvious.

In Pillar II, the pension funds were created without any security capital backing them. This is not a problem in the accumulation phase, since these institutions undertake no special risks or guarantees. But when it comes to the annuity phase, it is an important defect. For this reason, pension funds should be left out of the circle of annuity providers, which should consist entirely of existing or newly founded (possibly by the pension fund) life insurance companies, or specialized annuity insurance companies that possess the adequate security guarantees. In the case of the pension funds, there is only one benefit that can be provided without any undue difficulty: namely, the regular withdrawal of money from the fund account before the commencement of a two-person annuity. The regulations may state that this benefit can only be provided by the pension funds (naturally under Pillar II).

Also under Pillar II, the state has to set up a "final provider" if the pension funds are excluded from the circle of institutions that provide annuities. The final provider is necessary because it could, in theory, happen that there is no institution willing to provide an annuity on the free market (of course, the probability of this happening is theoretical). For the final provider, it is enough if the state declares that it will establish such an institution if nobody is willing voluntarily to provide an annuity for the pensioners of Pillar II.

Relationship between the Pension System and Other Systems

Here we have to examine the dependants', the disability, and the health subsystems. The two elements of the dependants' subsystem, the widow/er's and the orphan's benefits, wouldhave to behave in different ways. With the design of Pillar I and Pillar II set out above, there is no need to set up a separate widow/er's benefit system, since for married couples the total pension saving and the pension benefit itself (allowing for the divorce and inheritance rules) are for all intents and purposes considered to be the couple's "joint venture". Within this joint venture, the division of labour can be determined freely by the couple and has no effect on their benefits. So, if the division of labour within the family is such that the wife has no paying job, but runs the household and raises the children, she does not miss out on a pension if she divorces or if her husband dies, because, as a right as the spouse, she automatically receives old age benefits, in an actuarially correct and accountable way (and in the case of younger widows, there is no justification for the wider risk community having to provide for them).

Thus the benefit subsystem for dependants includes only orphan's benefit. We propose separating this and the disability subsystem from both pillars, and forming independent subsystems (either the two together, or separately), with independent contributions and benefit payments. Regarding the orphan's benefit, the first question is who should be considered as the risk community. There are basically two options:

1. every contribution payer;
2. only those with dependent children.

If we consider the principle of actuarial correctness, then both of these alternatives are very rough and ready. In reality, society must think more carefully who, in the end, should bear the burden and the expense of raising children, and should create an orphan's benefit system accordingly. Without these careful observations (which, though we indicate the need for them, do not fit into the framework of this book), we can give only a rough answer as to the level of the orphan's benefit and the composition of the risk community. However, children are needed by the whole society, and so, when they are orphaned, raising them should be the business of the whole society; thus the risk community should be "every contribution payer".

It is almost exclusively in their active employment phase that parents die leaving orphans, and so the need for orphan's benefit correlates well with the number of active people in the population. Consequently, the orphan's benefit can be organized on a pay-as-you-go basis, where the annual amount of the annuity paid to current orphans is added (together with the other contributions) as a separate orphans' contribution on the active.

In many respects, the same goes for disability benefit. It should be organized separately from both pension pillars, and a separate, designated contribution should be assigned to it. Naturally, the practice of improving the lot of the unemployed by paying them disability benefit has to be stopped. (By the simple expedient of naming every phenomenon and handling problems directly at source!) Leaving aside this current practice, the number of disabled again correlates well with the number of active (since we still suggest that only those in the active age should be considered disabled), so the provision for them can readily be organized, even theoretically,[71] in a pay-as-you-go system. The cover of the annual disability benefits paid should be laid on the active as a designated disability contribution.

It is important that we should always regard disability as reversible: it cannot be the goal either of the individual himself or of the state for someone to remain disabled. But this has the consequence that, during disability, care must be taken to ensure that old age pension contributions are kept up. The way to do this is to make the disability pension a gross amount, in the sense that it also contains the cover for contributions to be paid into Pillar I and Pillar II – and these, really, do have to be paid into both fund accounts. If someone recovers from disability before he reaches the average retirement age, then the disability annuity is terminated, and he goes on to receive an annuity from Pillar I and Pillar II, according to the general principles. It is also useful to calculate the annuity for the disabled using a more favourable annuity table, since their remaining life expectancy will be shorter than the population average.

We envisage indexation of both the orphan's and the disability benefits occurring in the same way as indexation of the fund accounts of Pillar I, i.e. using the gross wage index.

Currently, the dependency and disability risks are also handled within Pillar I of the pension system. These absorb a significant portion of the budget of the Central Administration of National Pension Insurance, as the following table shows.

Table 60. Necessary level of contribution by risk (%)

	1997	1998	1999	2000	2001
Old age	21.5	22.0	22.1	20.8	20.3
Disability	9.0	9.1	9.2	8.7	8.6
Dependency	4.2	4.7	4.7	4.3	4.1

Source: Réti 2002.

At the same time, the table does provide a starting point for determining how the unified contribution should initially be split between the three benefit subsystems (old age pension, disability, and orphan's).

The pension system and the health system are connected at several points. It is well known that certain jobs are harmful to the health of the employee and increase health expenditures, but since they decrease the life expectancy, they also mean lower pension expenditures. As they undertake health reform, many countries try to nudge the health system towards actuarial correctness and transparent financial accounting. The ageing of the population presents a challenge, since it is well known that the health expenditures on an ageing population is higher than that of a younger population. We must also be prepared for this, and in any reform of the healthcare system, there must be sufficient funds to to provide dignified healthcare for the elderly.

The above step is naturally only the first in the reform of the healthcare system, since contribution payments are still proportional to income rather than need; but the above reform means that contribution payments and expenditure might be balanced, at least at the level of age groups.

In the process of the reform of the health system described above, the key element is the general introduction of long-term health savings, since it is a special feature of healthcare that its benefits are least needed when the individual is earning the most (i.e. in the active phase), and are most needed when the individual no longer has wage income (i.e. in old age). This conundrum has to be solved the same way as for pensions – through advance saving – so connection of the two systems in this way is plausible. Reform of the healthcare system could be started in the same way as reform of the pension system, through voluntary long-term saving for healthcare purposes, and with the introduction of medical savings accounts. This would bring the issue onto the population's radar, and would get them used to a different kind of funding – one that is more correct and economically more stable.

Switch to the New System

The switch to the system described above must begin with a profound and wide-ranging debate, followed by legislation. Legislation must provide an adequate transitional timeframe, which means that changes should only affect those who are able to prepare for the effects of the change. For all other classes and age groups, the current system must remain unchanged. Of course, it is untenable for several systems with a different logic to exist alongside one another for any length of time; so for new entrants to the labour market, the new system should be compulsory. Moreover, we believe that a wide range of people currently active could also be switched to the new system without any great shock.

There is a definite date – still a little way off – when the current pension system will undergo radical change: 1 January 2013. From that date on, anyone who retires with a private pension fund will have to purchase an annuity from the amount accumulated in the private pension fund. It would be sensible to time the bigger change that is proposed to coincide with this date. That means 1 January 2013 would be the date from which anyone who retires from Pillar I would have his new-style annuity calculated. Of course, the features of the annuity benefit should be set down in law over the next few years, so that providers (in Pillar II, as well as the social security system in Pillar I) can prepare for it, as well as the insured. The current widow's pension system would also be in effect up to this date.

It is essential that those entitlements already acquired during the transition should not suffer. In theory, there are two possible ways to handle entitlements acquired before the introduction of the new pension system:

1. have these entitlements built in to the new pension system, with the old entitlements serving as a starting point for the new system;
2. have the old and the new systems handle the entitlements acquired in the two systems differently.

The first approach is based on a kind of opening balance of the new fund account – in other words, we would calculate an initial value according to past contribution payments. There are various ways of calculating the initial value: either we could calculate a concrete fund value, or we could calculate an initial pension segment that will be rolled forward later on.

The second approach is based on the two systems operating independently: even though one system is closed to new money, the pensions it continues to pay are treated independently of the new system. We can look at it in much the same way as pension entitlements from different countries of the EU are calculated, where, on retirement, the pension annuity is calculated from two separate pension systems.

We should be clear, though, that the Hungarian pension system has only collected contribution information since 1988, and the system is non-linear in many respects. Because of this, converting the acquired pension entitlements to fund value or initial pension level, and then closing the current system is perilous for several reasons. On the one hand, for those who paid contributions prior to 1988, it is difficult to correctly determine the total contributions actually paid; on the other hand, the value of the initial pension segment cannot easily be calculated because of the non-linear calculation. Closing the old system according to the first approach gives rise to constitutional misgivings and is a very large-scale undertaking, so there is an argument for counting the entitlements from the two systems together, but separately.

The fund accounts of Pillar I could be set up in 1 to 1.5 years. These would have to be set up for everyone who will turn 62 after 1 January 2013. For anyone older than this, the current system would continue to apply. The old rules would still apply to a fund owner who retires before 1 January 2013.

The pension contributions actually paid into Pillar I will be recorded on the fund account. The period before the account is set up could be handled in a dual way:

1. From 1988, the social security system has precise records of the contribution payments of each individual. These payments would be credited to each account, correcting the payments in each year by the gross wage index for the appropriate time period.
2. The payments that were made before 1988 would have to be estimated.

This estimate would have to consider several rules:

1. The contributions made in the non-documented period have to be estimated from the contributions made in the documented period – of course, these likewise would have to be corrected by the gross wage index of the appropriate period.
2. Within a given period (e.g. two years), every insured has the right to show that his actual contribution payments were higher than estimated. In this case, the amount credited would have to be corrected.
3. In the case of those who are at least 47, the amount credited must be adjusted if, at the time of crediting, the fund value is less than the insured would have received under the old system.

Although this method could be disputed on several points, one of its great advantages is that it closes the current pension system within a reasonable time. Because of the complexity of our pension system, we think it is worth considering the second alternative, too. That means the past and the future systems would operate separately, with the entitlements earned under the old system are not transferred to the new system. Instead, the pension would be determined on the basis of entitlements earned under two different systems that are independent of one another. (Just as is customary in the case of entitlements earned in two different countries of the European Union.)

The separation of the fund in case of divorce, and inheritance by the widow (or the risk group if there is no widow), must be introduced when the new system is set up. At the same time as the fund account is introduced to Pillar I, the new rules governing divorce and inheritance have to be introduced in Pillar II.

At this time – or in fact preferably earlier – contributions must be subdivided into pension, disability and orphan's contributions. Similarly, the new-style disability and orphan's benefits should be introduced at the latest when the fund accounts are set up, though this could happen earlier.

Institutional and Legislative Background

There is no need for new institutions to realize the new system. The institutions of Pillar II are already in existence, so it is only the regulation that has to be modified. Of the institutions, it is the functioning of the Central Administration of National Pension Insurance, which currently runs Pillar I, that has to be changed the most. This is necessary because, in the future, the following sub-elements have to be clearly separated (either by having separate institutions created, or within the current single institution):

1. the "old" system until it runs out;
2. Pillar 0;
3. the reformed Pillar I;
4. the orphan's benefit;
5. disability benefits.

It is not necessary to list all the modifying legal provisions at this stage, but we would like to outline a few points that have only been briefly mentioned in the discussion so far.

We suggest that the government should put some very general guarantees behind the system. One of the most important assurances is that it should guarantee repayment of the amount accumulated in the funds (by repayment, naturally we mean only repayment methods prescribed by law) – i.e. it should basically be recognized as state debt. Another government assurance would be that the nominal value of pensions paid as annuities cannot decrease on account of regular mortality changes.

We have painted a picture of a flexible pension system – a system in which retirement is not as cut and dried as it is today, since the pension can be suspended and restarted, and generally there is a wide range of parameters for retirement from which the insured himself can select. This means the tax system must also be modified. Pensions cannot be considered a special form of income, so the pension annuity must be included in the income tax base. Of course, this means that the contribution cannot be taxed, since then the same income would be taxed twice.

Possible Further Development of the System

We have already referred several times to possible improvement of the system. We think the most important improvement would be the gradual funding of Pillar I (most likely accomplished over several decades) – that is, first gradually turning the implicit state debt behind Pillar I into explicit debt, and then (also gradually) making it disappear as state debt. There are basically two possible ways of achieving this:
1. gradually decreasing the weight of Pillar I compared to Pillar II;
2. funding within Pillar I.

The big advantage of funding is that it relieves the active age groups of the burden of currently having to provide for older generations, and makes the level of pension more certain, as it does not depend on possibly unfavourable demographic trends. Funding also makes it possible for the benefits of the pension system to flow to the beneficiaries through a channel other than the government budget, which has the effect of decreasing the load on the latter.

The argument against funding always boils down to the same thing, and this is something we must seriously consider. This argument is that the level of pensions is exposed to the sometimes highly volatile capital markets, and uncertainty of this magnitude is not acceptable in such a fundamental institution of social security. For our part, we admit that the calculability of pensions is a very important factor, but we would qualify this by saying that the significance of calculability decreases as the average level of pensions increases. Thus low pensions cannot bear volatility, but the higher the pension, the greater the oscillations of the actual level can be. This way of thinking is important, as it can inform the extent to which the load is shifted from Pillar I to Pillar II – that is, how far the fund accounts can be transferred to Pillar II.

But then, nor is Pillar II exposed to capital market volatility, either. Such volatility can largely be avoided by using derivative products. Since these are not necessarily available, the government may have to release them – in return, of course, for an adequate (market-based) fee. This system is much more correct and more attuned to market logic than the current private fund guarantee system.

The state of being non-funded is not the only scenario under which Pillar I can avoid exposure to capital market volatility. This could also be the case if the system is funded, but the insured do not receive their pension direct from the fund. It is possible that the state could establish fund-managing trustees, whose managed fund would gradually reach the mass of implicit state debt on the fund accounts; these trustees would not invest in the government's own papers. In this case, the debt of the state behind the pensions is totally covered, though it is questionable whether the yield of the fund managed by the trustees would be as great as the government's pension expenditure. In a sense, this is unimportant. What is important is that, in this kind of construction, the fund handled by the state trustees should almost totally relieve the government budget of current pension expenditure. The role of the budget would be reduced to having to bolster the yield of trustees in bad years; this money would then be returned when the capital market had good years.

That said, the state itself is not the best fund-managing trustee! For this reason, we are in favour of Pillar II gradually becoming stronger and taking over from Pillar I, with yields equalized by derivatives.

THE ENVIRONMENT AND EFFECT OF THE PENSION SYSTEM AND AN ALTERNATIVE TO IT

It is fairly common to describe the economy of a country in terms of its GDP per capita. From this perspective, Hungary is at the end of the list of developed countries. In many respects, a more important indicator is the size of capital accumulated, especially as working and fixed capital of enterprises. By this measure, Hungary is rather further adrift of the developed countries, which has the evident result that our economy is strongly dependent on capital import, and we are exposed to the transient interests of the capital imported from other countries. It is evident that a greater volume of "domestic" capital automatically attached to the country would place the Hungarian economy in a less exposed situation; moreover – depending on the size of the capital – we could even move from being an exposed country to one that makes the running. This requires an economic policy that stimulates domestic capital accumulation. And the most obvious way to do this is to make the pension system funded.

It is not necessary, though, to invest the total accumulated pension fund in Hungary, since Hungarian capital abroad increases Hungary's (and its people's) economic power. Of course, for this to work, the foreign investments should not be sporadic and disjointed, but possibly all part of a kind of Hungarian economic strategy. The pension fund – because of its concentrated character – is well suited to creating a strategy in this sense.

The pension fund should be used for a certain regional expansion of the Hungarian economy. Funding the pension system is not enough for this: it has to be allied to an economic policy that helps the investment of accumulated capital. This means the development of the capital market, where a lot of new Hungarian ideas can find the capital they need, allowing these new enterprises (or some of them) to grow into big, strong Hungarian enterprises, maybe even regional multinational companies. Economic policy should explicitly set this as a target.

As a matter of fact, we could extend the idea of funding as a requirement from the pension system through to almost any long-term state liability. We could say that a well-functioning state has no debts, and that all its liabilities are covered. Of course, this could only be set as a target, since, from time to time, the state may find an important pan-society target (e.g. building motorways) that could be viewed basically as a pan-society investment worthy of indebtedness. But efforts should be made to keep these events rare and truly justified. In other words, the investment characteristic of the liability must be verifiable and must warrant expenditure right across society.

The indebtedness of the state narrows the future potential of the economy, since repayment will need increased tax revenue, which could be viewed as capital withdrawal. For this reason, the need for indebtedness should be carefully thought through. Current outstanding debt should be consciously cut down, and the state should not allow pension funds to invest their money in government bonds over the long term.

One of the non-negligible social effects of a mature funded pension system is that it lifts most of the citizens of the country in question out of their economically subservient position and makes them "capitalist" in a sense – which means they occupy a far less subservient position economically. The funded pension system "frees" current retirees, since the fact that they become "capitalists" means, at the same time, that they no longer depend for their pension on the "grace" of those currently active.

The effect of this on the whole country would be that Hungary ceases to depend so heavily on foreign capital, and instead other countries come to depend, to some extent, on Hungary..

The Environment Required by Funded Systems

A funded system does not function well simply by virtue of being funded. The system itself must be carefully constructed, but it also has to have an appropriate environment. Luckily, the environment needed is not specific to the pension system, but is needed generally for a well-functioning economy. Let us consider the elements in turn.

Created by the State

Regulating the Retirement Age – Relativization

Regulating, relativizing the retirement age, is an integral part of the concept. Relativizing the retirement age is also important in forestalling the impending labour force shortfall, as it offers a way of encouraging employment in old age. The improving health of the population enables this, but many obstacles of attitude, legislation and education have to be cleared out of the way. One is the notion that retirement implies an absolute break with employment. Clearing the other obstacles is also the duty of the state. For example, retraining, part-time work, etc., should be made more widely available.

Solidarity between Genders

In state-controlled pension systems it is a self-evident triviality, not worthy of discussion, that – assuming the same fund and the same age – men and women receive the same initial annuity. In private insurance practice, though, this is self-evidently not the case: in Hungary, for example, life expectancy at birth is approximately 10 years lower for men than for women, and the mortality advantage of women is maintained throughout life. Thus the correct practice would be to use different annuity tables for men and women in the state pension systems, too.

If we go deeper into the problem, we see that this question cannot be answered quickly or easily, since the use of a uniform, unisex annuity table compensates for a lot of hidden social inequalities. Thus repealing the unisex annuity table in the long term must be considered (if it is allowed at all by EU directives), but this can only be done if, at the same time, the inequalities facing women are systematically uncovered and rectified. To take just a few examples: women are still not equal on the labour market: they do not always get the same wage for the same job. Typically they tend to be concentrated in fields that do not pay well and where wages are unfairly low (e.g. education, public health). Through marriage, they typically live in economic communities with men, where formal income is mostly attributed to men; however, when we examine the internal division of labour between them (e.g. child-care this income could be viewed as property acquired in common, on which the spouse would also have to pay pension contributions, etc.

On an even wider horizon, employing a uniform annuity table in reality means that income flows not only from men to women, but generally from classes of higher mortality to classes of lower mortality. Some of these directions of flow are:
- from the sick to the healthy;
- from the poor to the wealthy;
- from rural to urban;
- from smokers to non-smokers.

In the long run, these redistributions also have to be systematically surveyed and gradually stopped. While this is being done, it should not be forgotten that there may be an opposite redistribution in other subsystems of the social security system, so together they may balance each other out – e.g. in the public health system, non-smokers certainly partly finance the more expensive treatment of smokers.

Necessary Institutions

The funded pension system cannot function without a properly functioning capital market. Thus the state must do its utmost to stimulate the development and adequate functioning of the capital market. This covers supervision, economic legislation, accounting regulation and an economic policy that prefers the development of officially quoted national enterprises as well. Of course, convertibility of the local currency and adequate openness of the economy are fundamental prerequisites.

The state must encourage the development of a clear and supervised market for all properties of great value. Accordingly, up-to-date and secure real estate and apartment registers must be created. The mobility of real estate property, apartment block construction and the incidence of apartment rental must be stimulated, as this also encourages mobility of the labour force. The elderly should be enabled to sell their large apartments that they no longer require and to move into sheltered developments for the elderly. Legislation must be passed in this field, and the "annuity for apartment" movement must be placed on a business footing.[71]

Other State-Controlled Subsystems That Must Be in Tune with the Pension System

The most important subsystem in this respect is the tax system (mainly the personal income tax system), which should support the pension system. The main elements of an income tax system that is in tune with our proposed pension system are:
- A tax-free band up to the subsistence level.
- The total pension contribution imposed on the gross income of the employee (although a certain wage-proportional solidarity tax could be imposed on employers).

- The base of personal income tax is the gross income, decreased by the pension and health insurance contributions – that is, the source of pension savings is the tax-free income.
- When the annuity commences, it is totally part of the income tax base; but then the pension contribution is not paid any more (only the health insurance contribution). This means the tax base is higher, but the total tax and contribution payable is relatively lower. This way there is no counter-incentive for employment after retirement, and the tax system is correct and clear.

The state as a final guarantor

Even in a totally funded pension system there is a need for government intervention; but the nature (and degree) of it is far removed from the current situation. Instead of formally organizing the payment of pensions, the state can entrust this to independently managed institutions. The state must organize the supervision of these institutions.

Naturally, there may be smaller or larger fluctuations in the economy, when the value of pension funds dips significantly, and so does the level of annuities payable. In certain extraordinary situations, a dip may need to trigger some (strictly temporary) government intervention, when pensions are topped up by public funds. But interventions like this must be rare, and the system must pay back the money that the government has pumped into the system. So the role of the state here is to offer a kind of ultimate guarantee and to even out large fluctuations due to economic downturns.

It would be wise to preclude the necessity for such government intervention. As we have already mentioned, this could be done institutionally, through the release of government derivatives.

Of course, the state is necessary to operate the support system (mostly on a pay-as-you-go basis), since in every compulsory system there will always be some whose savings are not even enough to purchase a subsistence-level pension. But this pay-as-you-go system must be smaller than the current system by several orders of magnitude, and government social policy must seek to have far smaller groups needing this support at all (particularly by encouraging education and retraining).

International Environment

Portability

In the case of the international environment, there are two directions of expectation. Not only can the funded pension system "feel better" in one international environment than in another, but the international environment can also have expectations of the pension system.

The most important condition – latent as yet, but already perceptible – expected by the international environment is that pensions become portable. Portability means that if an employee works in different countries during his career – which, with the advent of the EU, is becoming more and more common – he can collect the pension entitlements acquired in different countries without difficulty, and in the end it doesn't matter in what country he retires. On the system level, we can say that portability requires the pension systems that the employee comes into contact with during his career, have to be transparent and be able to communicate with each other.

Funded pension systems are fundamentally open systems, and can communicate with each other without any difficulty. Communication between funded systems is simple: just as an employee can switch to a different pension fund within the country by taking the fund accumulated on his account with him, the same can be done with the pension funds of different countries (moreover the employee may not even have to do this, since pension funds can quite naturally be international). Transfer between pay-as-you-go systems, on the other hand, has to be regulated by complex bilateral international agreements that are not always correct. One example is the international agreement between the Hungarian and the Romanian pay-as-you-go systems. Under this agreement, the country in which a resettled employee lives at retirement has to pay the total pension. We leave it up to the reader to decide whether this agreement benefits both countries equally or burdens one country disproportionately.[72] It is clear, then, that, in a correct settling of accounts, the individual would take the implicit state debt with him. That is, in these cases, the state from which the individual is moving would release explicit debt bonds,[73] and hand the bonds over to the pension system of the other country. It should not come as a surprise that there are no such agreements:

1. Generally the pension reserve is not recorded at the level of the individual.
2. No pay-as-you-go pension system is prepared to handle the state debt bond of another country.

As we mentioned earlier, it will become objectively more and more uncertain which citizen belongs to which country within the European Union. One of the most important assumptions underpinning the pay-as-you-go system has begun to be revealed for what it is – wrong. Namely, that the population of a country is stable, it does not "move" back and forth during its career, so the closed pension system can be based on this secure footing. With the formation of the European Union, these closed systems get in the way of free movement and are a means of binding the people to one particular country.

A Useful Pension Strategy for the EU

One can easily see that the motley collection of mainly closed pay-as-you-go-type European pension systems, which are incompatible with each other, will soon come to be a source of strife and will strongly hinder European integration. Because of this, their overall reform should be put on the agenda. Naturally, reform of systems of this size and importance can only happen very slowly and with great caution. As a first step, the most important thing is to clarify the situation. The introduction of the fund account system could greatly contribute to this. Thus – in our view – the expedient way of undertaking pension system reform in the EU is:

Step 1: make the fund account system everywhere compulsory, and in this way uncover hidden redistribution and state debt.

Step 2: the state debt behind the fund account system should be written to other state debt and treated together.

Step 3: generally prescribe a low level of state debt, which means that the funding of the system must be started (i.e. the reserve must be transferred from government bonds to other instruments).

Since Pillar II already exists in most European countries, gradually emptying Pillar I and shifting the benefits to Pillar II should no longer cause a problem.

International Diversification of Investments

It is expedient to internationally diversify the reserve behind funded systems. This point of view may be surprising to some, since it seems straightforward that pension funds are ordered to keep a certain portion of their investments in government bonds, and the rest in national stock or national bonds in order to help strengthen the national economy. We have already discussed government bonds. It is not effective to have too many of these in circulation, because it means state indebtedness, which is not a natural, favourable situation. And if the state is not indebted, pension funds cannot invest in government bonds, even if they are regulated to do so. Of course, the repayment of existing state debt can only be accomplished over a lengthy period of time, and so it is conceivable to have a – temporary – regulation allowing the investment of part of the reserves in government bonds. But this must – consciously – be only temporary!

Ordering national investment for a period of time may be justified for as long as the country has a relative lack of capital. But as the pension reserves increase, this problem gradually ceases to exist, and the problem of security crops up. International diversification is a solution to this.

The problem of security has two dimensions:

1. a war or crisis striking at a certain geographical area;
2. the unfavourable demographic tendencies of a certain geographical area.

As we saw earlier, one of the main reasons for the development of pay-as-you-go systems was that the reserves behind funded systems were destroyed during World War II. And it was the fear that they would be destroyed once more that got in the way of the systems being funded again later. Geographical diversification provides a solution to this problem. Of course, this is not a panacea, since it provides no protection against a catastrophe striking the whole world; but it does give protection against local hyperinflation, a localized war, etc.

The unfavourable demographic tendencies almost enforce geographical diversification. If the number of retirees in a country is significantly higher than the number of active people – and most European countries are heading this way – then, after a while, the active population simply cannot make enough capital work for its yield to provide also for the retirees. The solution is to invest in countries with more favourable demographic indicators.

Naturally, international diversification also has its dangers so, with such unfavourable demographic trends, economic policy has to aim at two things:

1. promoting home employment of the aged as much as possible;
2. promoting the use of capital-intensive technologies, so that being dependent on foreign countries does not mean defencelessness, and so that there is an alternative.

As we have seen, if we focus in on Hungary, then the foreign investment of pension funds causes a kind of parity: it puts Hungarian pensioners in the same situation as the pensioners of developed Western countries: not only do Western pensioners – through their pension funds – have a stake in Hungary, but similarly Hungarian pensioners would have a stake abroad. It is beneficial if Hungary's relationship to the West, and generally to other countries, is not one-sidedly dependent – with them as the proprietors and us as the workmen – but balanced; and this requires significant foreign investment of Hungarian capital.

International Stability, Economic Prosperity

Since international diversification is important in itself, it is also important that this diversification should be objectively secure. Investments should only be made in economically and politically stable countries, where legal security is developed, and where there is no barrier to international commerce, capital flow, etc. As far as the pension system is concerned, it is desirable if there are many prosperous economies and if there is peace. This is especially true of those countries where demographic trends are favourable, since it is most effective if the pension capital of ageing countries is invested there.

Long-Term Problems

According to today's logic, the funded systems must contend with two problems that are of very long duration worldwide. The very long term means several generations, so that does not affect the introduction of the funded system today. These problems are:
1. if demographic trends are unfavourable throughout the world;
2. we do not have information on whether there are enough profitable investments throughout the world for funding of the large western pension systems.

When we spokeof unfavourable demographic trends, we have consistently meant low birth rates, increasing life expectancy and an increased proportion of aged people in the population. Of course, these trends are only "unfavourable" in terms of the pension system: in other respects they are very favourable. Everybody wants an increase in life expectancy; lower birth rates are a fundamental condition for environmental protection and the survival of the world, and the (temporary) ageing is the logical consequence of this. Moreover the "unfavourable demographic trends" within a country are only unfavourable for the pay-as-you-go scheme: they make no difference to a funded scheme. If these trends were to appear throughout the world, then they may affect funded systems, too, since then the countries of aged population could not find a country with a young population in which to invest and reap the benefits for the pension funds. There are two ways of protecting against this still quite distant threat – as we mentioned earlier:

1. gradually shifting from labour-intensive to capital-intensive production (at the current stage of automatization this does not seem a particularly difficult task)
2. gradually drawing groups of aged people – whose physical and mental state will, of course, constantly be improving – more and more into production, changing the direction of current tendencies of the labour market.

As for the possibility of profitable investments, we cannot give an answer. That remains known only to the future!

An Alternative to the Pension System

As a general rule, the pension system protects us against poverty caused by a decreased capacity for work. But it is not the pension system, nor the state, that affords us the greatest protection from poverty – it is wealth. A wealthy man does not need a pension. Thus, if the state wants to combat poverty, then it is not the pension system that primarily needs to be developed (although this will also be inevitable for some considerable time to come); instead, it needs to throw all its weight behind enrichment, behind its citizens' accumulation of wealth. Perhaps people wealthy enough could even be let out of the mandatory pension system (though of course they could not be relieved of the solidaristic contribution to the support system).

In a funded system, it is the task of the government to even out possible large fluctuations in the level of pensions. But this is only necessary if pensioners do not have significant property-proportional income. If a significant part of the population has significant property, then this "guarantor-type" function of the state can be reduced.

For this to come about, it must be a target of economic policy. One very important element is the tax system. The tax system must be constructed so as to encourage accumulation and make current consumption less attractive. That is: big taxes should fundamentally be imposed on consumption, to make consumption expensive. But taxes related to the accumulation of property – except inheritance – should be scrapped, e.g. real estate stamp duty and profit tax; by contrast, anything that involves consuming accumulated wealth (e.g. selling an apartment) should be significantly taxed.

Buying a car is not considered accumulation of wealth, so that activity should also have significant consumption tax attached to it.

Inheritance (and donation) tax – above a certain level of wealth – may be strongly progressive, since the state not only has to promote wealth in itself, but also the activity of acquiring property. The goal of accumulating wealth is to provide long-term personal security, to help with raising the next generation, and to enrich society. In order to enable the next generation to acquire wealth on their own, they must be given the chance. Of course, inheritance tax can be offset in exchange for donations and expenditure in the public interest.

GLOSSARY OF TERMS

Actuarial correctness:
The premium of an insurance with a given benefit, or the benefits corresponding to a given premium are determined after precisely examining the individual risks in such a way that the stochastic equivalence of premiums paid and benefits received individually holds.

Defined Benefit (DB) system:
A (mostly pension) system in which the insured are told in advance, on the basis of some principle such as the number of working years and the average wage, what benefits they will be entitled to in their pensioner years. In DB systems, the contributions paid by the insured depend only loosely on the expected benefits.

Defined Contribution (DC) system:
This term covers a (mostly pension) system in which payments by the insured (members) are precisely registered in an interest-earning account, and benefits are calculated at retirement according to the principle of individual equivalence, based on the capital accumulated on the individual account. The Hungarian pension funds function in a defined contribution system.

Fund account system:
The term covers the English Notionally Defined Contribution (NDC) system. It fundamentally means a defined contribution-type pay-as-you-go system.

Implicit state debt:
The present value of liabilities undertaken by the state that, though not formally accounted as state debt, can be calculated. The state guarantee behind a pay-as-you-go pension system is a typical implicit state debt.

Pay-as-you-go system:
Originally the financing method of a risk community in which the members of the risk community divided up among themselves the loss consequent upon an event, and paid their share of the loss to the risk-community member who suffered the loss. Today the term is mostly used in connection with pension systems. It is used in the sense that current expenditure (annuity benefits) is covered by current income (contribution payments), and long-term reserves are not built up at all (or only to a small degree).

Pillar I:
A term whose meaning varies from country to country. In Hungary it means the state-organized pay-as-you-go pension system.

Pillar II:
The term usually covers a compulsory, funded pension subsystem based on individual savings. In Hungary it refers to the system of private pension funds.

Private fund:
An institution of Pillar II – a self-governing, non-profit institution, owned by its members, that runs the individual fund accounts of the members, collects their compulsory pension savings and invests them. The official term is "private pension fund", but here we use the shorthand "private fund".

Solidarity:
In economic terms, this means income redistribution, i.e. taking money away from those who have (relatively) plenty and giving it to those who lack it. In pension systems, it primarily means redistributing annuities from men to women and from high-contribution payers to low-contribution payers.

Unisex annuity table:
An annuity premium table in which, notwithstanding the great difference in their remaining life expectancy, there is no difference between the premiums of men and women.

REFERENCES

Aaron, H. J. (1996): The Social Insurance Paradox, *Canadian Journal of Economics and Political Science* 32: 371–74.

Aaron, Henry J. and Reischauer Robert D. (1998): *Countdown to Reform: The Great Social Security Debate*. New York: The Century Foundation Press.

Advisory Council on Social Security (1997): Report of the 1994–1996 Advisory Council on Social Security. Washington, DC: US Government Printing Office.

Antal, K., Réti, J.and Toldi, M. (1995): Nyugdíjak értékvesztése, *Munkaügyi Szemle* 39, 12: 14–22.

Arrow, K. J. (1963): Uncertainty and the Welfare Economics of Medical Care, *American Economic Review* 53: 941–69.

Auerbach, A. J., Hagemann, R. P., Kotlikoff, L. J.and Nicoletti, G. (1989): The Economic Dynamics of an Ageing Population: The Case of Four OECD Countries, *OECD Economic Studies 12*: 97–130.

Auerbach, A. J. and Herrmann, H. (eds) (2002): *Ageing, Financial Markets and Monetary Policy*. Berlin: Springer.

Augusztinovics, M. (1999): Nyugdíjrendszerek és reformok az átmeneti gazdaságokban, *Közgazdasági Szemle* 46: 657–72.

Augusztinovics, M. (2000): Újraelosztás nyugdíjbiztosítási rendszerekben. In: M. Augusztinovics (ed.), *Körkép reform után: Tanulmányok a nyugdíjrendszerről*. Budapest: Közgazdasági Szemle Alapítvány, pp. 318–39.

Balogh, G. (1996): *Társadalombiztosítási ismeretek. Bevezetés a társadalombiztosításba*. Zsámbék: Corvinus Kiadó.

Balogh, G. and Szűcs, L. (1998): *Alkalmazott társadalombiztosítás-tan (társadalombiztosítási jog és alkalmazása)*. Budapest: Osiris Kiadó.

Banks, J., Disney, R. and Smith, Z. (2000): What can we learn from Generational Accounts for the United Kingdom? *Economic Journal Features* 110, November: F575–F597.

Banyár, J. (2003): *Életbiztosítás*. Budapest, Aula.

Barr, N. (1987): *The Economics of the Welfare State*. London: Weidenfeld and Nicolson/Stanford University Press.

Barr, N. (2000): Reforming Pensions: Myths, Truths and Policy Choices. IMF Working Paper No. WP/00/139. Washington, DC: IMF.

Barr, N. (2001): *The Welfare State as a Piggy Bank: Information, Risk, Uncertainty and the Role of the State*. Oxford: Oxford University Press.

Blejer, M. I. and Cheasty, A. (1991): The Measurement of Fiscal Deficits: Analytical and Methodological Issues, *Journal of Economic Literature* 29, December: 1644–78.

Bohn, H. (1992): Budget Deficits and Government Accounting. In: A. Meltzer and C. Plosser (eds), *Carnegie–Rochester Conference Series on Public Policy* 36, July: 1–84.

Börsch-Supan, A. (1998): Incentive Effects of Social Security on Labor Force Participation: Evidence in Germany and Across Europe, National Bureau of Economic Research Working Paper 6780. Cambridge, MA

Börsch-Supan, A. (2001): Six Countries – And No Pension System Alike. In: A. Börsch-Supan and M. Miegel (eds), *Pension Reform in Six Countries*. Berlin: Springer, pp. 1–12.

Börsch-Supan, A. (2001): The German Retirement Insurance System. In: A. Börsch-Supan and M. Miegel (eds), *Pension Reform in Six Countries*. Berlin: Springer, pp. 13–38.

Börsch-Supan, A., Ludwig, A. and Winter, J. (2002): Aging, Pension Reform, and Capital Flows. In: A. J. Auerbach and H. Herrmann (eds): *Ageing, Financial Markets and Monetary Policy*. Berlin: Springer, pp. 55–83.

Buchanan, J. (1990): The Budgetary Politics of Social Security. In: C. Weaver (ed.), *Social Security's Looming Surpluses*. Washington, DC: American Enterprise Institute.

Catalan, M., Impavido, G. and Musalem, A. (2000): Contractual Savings or Stock Market Development: Which Leads? World Bank, Financial Sector Development Department (mimeo), July.

Central Statistics Office (CSO) (2001): *Demographic Yearbook*. Budapest.

Central Statistics Office (KSH) (2002): A Munkaerő-felmérés időszaki Adattár, 1992–2001 (Temporary data warehouse of labour force survey 1992–2001). Budapest.

Chand, S. and Jäger, A. (1996): Aging Populations and Public Pension Schemes, IMF Occasional Paper No. 147.

Chlon, A., Fox, L. and Palmer, E. (2002): Notional Defined Contribution Systems: How Are They Implemented? (Manuscript).

Cigno, A. (1991): *Economics of the Family*. Oxford: Clarendon Press.

Courbier S. (1999): Part-Time Work in Europe. In: D. Pieters (ed.), *Changing Work Patterns and Social Security*. EISS Yearbook. Kluwer: The Hague.

Czúcz, O. (1994): *Az öregségi nyugdíjrendszerek*. Budapest: Közgazdasági és Jogi Kiadó.

Daykin, C. (2000): Privately Managed Old-Age Pension Schemes: Theory and Reality. ISSA Working Paper.

Daykin, C. (2001): Unfunded Pensions in the EU and in the UK Public Sector. ISSA Working Paper.

Demény, P. (1987): Re-linking Fertility Behaviour and Economic Security in Old Age: A Pronatalist Reform, *Population and Development Review* 13, 1: 128–32

Diamond, Peter A. (1999): *Issues in Privatizing Social Security*. Cambridge, MA: The MIT Press for the National Academy of Social Insurance.

Diamond, Peter A., Geanakoplos, John, Mitchall, Olivia S. and Zeldes, Stephen P. (1998): Would a Privatized Social Security System Really Pay a Higher Return? In: Peter A. Diamond, A. Douglas Arnold, Michael J. Graetz and Alicia H. Munnell (eds.), *Framing the Social Security Debate: Values, Politics and Economics*. Washington, DC: Brookings Institution Press for the National Academy of Social Insurance.

Disney, R. (1996): *Can We Afford to Grow Older? A Perspective on the Economics of Aging*. Cambridge, MA: MIT Press.

Disney, R. (1999): Notional Accounts as a Pension Reform Strategy: An Evaluation. Social Protection Paper Series, Discussion Paper No. 9928, Washington, DC, World Bank.

Disney, R. (2000): Crises in Public Pension Programmes in OECD: What Are the Reform Options? *Economic Journal Features* 110, February: FI–F23.

Disney, R. (2000): Declining Public Pensions in an Era of Demographic Ageing: Will Private Provision Fill the Gap? *European Economic Review* 44: 4–6, 957–73.

Disney, R. and Whitehouse, E. (1999): Pension Plans and Retirement Incentives. Social Protection Paper Series, Discussion Paper No. 9924, Washington, DC, World Bank.

Economic Policy Committee (2000): Progress Report to the Ecofin Council on the Impact of Ageing Populations on Public Pension Systems. European Commission.

Economist (2002): A Survey of Pensions, *Economist*, February 16: 54ff.

Erikson, T. (2000): Reform of the Swedish Pension System. In: D. Pieters (ed), *Confidence and Changes*. EISS Yearbook. Kluwer: The Hague.

Esping-Andersen, G. (1990): *The Three Worlds of Welfare Capitalism*. Princeton: Princeton University Press.

European Commission (1996): *Employment in Europe*. Brussels/Luxembourg.

EUROSTAT (2000): *Living Conditions in Europe*.

Feldstein, M.(ed.) (1998): *Privatizing Social Security*. Chicago: University of Chicago Press.

Ferrera, M. (2001): European Integration and National Social Citizenship: Changing Boundaries, New Structuring? *Comparative Political Studies* 36, 6: 611–52.

Förster, M. and Pearson, M. (2000): *Income Distribution in OECD Countries*. OECD.

Fultz, E. (ed.) (2002): *Pension Reform in Central and Eastern Europe*. Budapest: ILO, vols. 1–2.

Gál, R. I., Simonovits, A. and Tarcali, D. (2000): Nyugdíjreform és korosztályi számla. In: M. Augusztinovics (ed.) *Körkép reform után: Tanulmányok a nyugdíjrendszerről*. Budapest: Közgazdasági Szemle Alapítvány, pp. 272–97.

Gál, R. I., Simonovits, A. and Tarcali, D. (2001): Nyugdíjreform és korosztályi számla, *Közgazdasági Szemle* 48: 291–306.

Greiner, D.(1999): Atypical Work in the EU. In: D. Pieters (ed.), *Changing Work Patterns and Social Security*. EISS Yearbook. Kluwer: The Hague.

Gruber, J. and Wise, D. (eds) (1999): *Social Security and Retirement Around the World*. National Bureau of Economic Research. Chicago: University of Chicago Press.

Gustafsson, S., Kenjoh, E. and Wetzels, C. (2000): New Crisis in European Population. In D. Pieters (ed.), *Confidence and Changes*. EISS Yearbook. Kluwer: The Hague.

Hassler, J. and Lindbeck, A. (1997): International Risk Sharing, Stability and Optimality of Alternative Pension Systems. Working Paper Series 493, University of Stockholm, Institute for International Economic Studies.

Holzmann, R. (1988): *Reforming Public Pensions*. Paris: OECD.

Holzmann, R. (1997): Pension Reform, Financial Market Development and Endogenous Growth-Preliminary Evidence for Chile. IMF Staff Papers, June, pp. 149–78.

Holzmann, R. (2000): The World Bank Approach to Pension Reform, *International Social Security Review* 53, 1: 11–34.

Holzmann, R. (2000): Can Investments in Emerging Markets Help to Solve the Aging Problem? Social Protection Paper Series, Discussion Paper No. 0010, March, Washington, DC, World Bank.

Holzmann, R. and Stiglitz, J. (eds) (2001): *New Ideas about Old-Age Security: Toward Sustainable Pension Systems in the 21st Century*. Washington, DC: World Bank.

Iglesias, A. and Palacios, R. (2001): Managing Public Pension Reserves: Evidence from the International Experience. In: R. Holzmann and J. Stiglitz (eds) (2001), *New Ideas about Old-Age Security: Toward Sustainable Pension Systems in the 21st Century*. Washington, DC: World Bank.

ILO (2000): *World Labour Report*. Geneva.

James, E., Smalhout, S. and Vittas, D. (2001): Administrative Costs and the Organization of Individual Account Systems: A Comparative Perspective. In: R. Holzmann and J. Stiglitz (eds) (2001), *New Ideas about Old-Age Security: Toward Sustainable Pension Systems in the 21st Century*. Washington, DC: World Bank.

Klosse, S. (2000): Social Protection: Public, Semi-Public or Private. In D. Pieters (ed.), *Confidence and Changes*. EISS Yearbook. Kluwer: The Hague.

Kotlikoff, L. (1996): Hogyan privatizáljuk a tb-nyugdíjrendszert, *Közgazdasági Szemle* 43: 1045–71.

Kotlikoff, L., Smetters, K. and Walliser, J. (1998): Opting Out of Social Security and Adverse Selection. NBER Working Paper Series, Working Paper 6430, February, Cambridge, MA.

Kruppe, T., Oschmiansky, H. and Schömann, K. (1998): Self-Employment: Employment Dynamics in the European Union, *informMISEP.* 64: 33–43.

Kune, J. (1996): The Hidden Liabilities: Meaning and Consequences. Revised version of a paper presented at the CBP Seminar Series, The Hague (mimeo).

Levine, R. (1997): Financial Development and Economic Growth – Views and Agenda, *Journal of Economic Literature* 35: 688–726.

Levine, R. and Zervos, S. (1996): Policy, Stock Market Development, and Long-Run Growth Part I, *The World Bank Economic Review* 10, 2: 323–39.

Lindbeck, A. and Weibull, J. (1988): Strategic Interaction with Altruism: The Economics of Fait Accompli, *Journal of Political Economy* 96: 1165–82.

Lindbeck, A. (2000): Pensions and Contemporary Socioeconomic Change. Seminar Paper 685, Stockholm University.

Lindbeck, A. and Persson, M. (2002): The Gains from Pension Reform. Seminar Paper 712, Stockholm University.

MISSOC-INFO (2001): *Old-age in Europe*. 01/2001. Brussels.

Müller, K. (1999): *The Political Economy of Pension Reform in Central-Eastern Europe*. Cheltenham, UK and Northampton, MA: Edward Elgar.

Munnel, Alicia H. and Balduzzi, Pierluigi (1998): Investing the Social Security Trust Funds in Equities. Public Policy Institute, American Association of Retired Persons, No. 9802 (March).

Murthi, Mamta, Orszag, Michael and Orszag, Peter R. (1999): Administrative Costs and Individual Accounts: Lessons from the UK Experience. World Bank (February).

OECD (1999): *Employment Outlook*. Paris.
OECD (2001): *Employment Outlook*. Paris.
OECD (2001): *Insurance and Private Pensions Compendium for Emerging Economies*. Paris.
OECD (2005): Pensions at a Glance, Public Policies across OECD Countries, Paris
Olsen, Kelly A. and Salisbury, Dallas L. (1998): Individual Social Security Accounts: Issues in Assessing Administrative Feasibility and Costs. Special Report and Issue Brief No. 203 (November).
ONYF (2000): *Statistical Yearbook*. Budapest.
ONYF (2001): *Statistical Yearbook*. Budapest.
Orszag, P. and Stiglitz, J. E. (2001): Rethinking Pension Reform: Ten Myths about Social Security Systems. In: R. Holzmann and J. Stiglitz (eds), *New Ideas about Old-Age Security: Toward Sustainable Pension Systems in the 21st Century*. Washington, DC: World Bank, pp. 17–56.
Palacios, R. and Whitehouse, E. (1999): The Role of Choice in the Transition to a Funded Pension System. Social Protection Paper Series, Discussion Paper No. 9812, Washington, DC, World Bank.
Palmer, E. (2000): The Swedish Pension Reform Model – Framework and Issues. Social Protection Paper Series, Discussion Paper No. 0012, Washington, DC, World Bank.
Pieters, D. (ed.) (1999): *Changing Work Patterns and Social Security*. EISS Yearbook. Kluwer: The Hague.
Pieters, D. (ed.) (2000): *Confidence and Changes*. EISS Yearbook. Kluwer: The Hague.
Réti, J. (2000): A kockázatok járulékterhei a kilencvenes évek végén (adalékok a magyar nyugdíjreform történetéhez). In: J. Király, A. Simonovits, and J. Száz (eds), *Racionalitás és méltányosság. Tanulmányok Augusztinovits Máriának*. Budapest: Közgazdasági Szemle Alapítvány, pp. 134–56.
Réti, J. (2002): A kockázatok járulékterhei. Manuscript.
Rofman, Rafael (2000): The Pension System in Argentina: Six Years after the Reform. Primer paper, June.
Roseveare, Deborah, Leibfritz, Willi, Fore, Douglas and Wurzel, Eckhard (1996): Ageing Populations, Pension Systems and Government Budgets: Simulations for 20 OECD Countries. Economics Department Working Paper No. 168. OECD.
Sandmo, A. (2003): Globalisation and the Welfare State: More Inequality, Less Redistribution? In: D. Pieters (ed.), *European Social Security and Global Politics*. Kluwer: The Hague.
Sarfati, H. and Bondi, G. (2002): *Labour Market and Social Protection Reforms in International Perspective*. Aldershot, UK: Ashgate.
Schmähl, A. (1999): Pension Reforms in Germany: Major Topics, Decisions and Developments. In: K. Müller, A. Ryll and H.-J. Wagener (eds), *Transformation of Social Security: Pensions in Central-Eastern Europe*. Heidelberg: Physica Verlag, pp. 91–120.
Schmähl, W., 2004: Paradigm Shift In German Pension Policy: Measures Aiming at a New Public-Private Mix and Their Effects. In: M. Rein and W. Schmähl (eds), *Rethinking the Welfare State – The Political Economy of Pension Reform*. Cheltenham, UK and Northampton, MA: Edward Elgar, pp. 153–204.

Schmid, G. (1997): The Dutch Employment Miracle? A Comparison of the Employment Systems in the Netherlands and Germany, *inforMISEP* 59: 23–31.

Simonovits, A. (1998): Az új magyar nyugdíjrendszer és problémái, *Közgazdasági Szemle* 45: 689–708.

Simonovits, A. (2001): Szolgálati idő, szabadidő és nyugdíj: ösztönzés korlátokkal, *Közgazdasági Szemle* 48: 291–306.

Stiglitz, J. E. (1988): *Economics of the Public Sector.* 2nd edition. New York and London: Norton. Revised Hungarian edition (2000): *A kormányzati szektor gazdaságtana.* Budapest: KJK.

Szabó, S. (2000): Nyugdíjrendszerünk 1929-től 1997-ig. In: M. Augusztinovics (ed.), *Körkép reform után: Tanulmányok a nyugdíjrendszerről.* Budapest: Közgazdasági Szemle Alapítvány, pp. 28–50.

Thompson, L. (1998): *Older and Wiser: The Economics of Public Pension,* Washington, DC: The Urban Institute Press.

United Nations Secretariat, Population Division, Department of Economic and Social Affairs (2000): *Replacement Migration: Is it a Solution to Declining and Ageing Populations?*

US Social Security Administration, Office of Policy, Office of Research Evaluation, and Statistics (1999): Social Security Programs Throughout the World 1999. SSA Publication No. 13-11805 (August).

Valdes-Prieto, S. (1997): *The Economics of Pensions: Principles, Policies and International Experience.* Cambridge: Cambridge University Press.

Valdes-Prieto, S. (2000): The Financial Stability of Notional Account Pensions, *Scandinavian Journal of Economics* 102, 3: 395–417

Walliser, J. (2001): Regulation of Withdrawals in Individual Account Systems. In R. Holzmann and J. Stiglitz (eds) (2001), *New Ideas about Old-Age Security: Toward Sustainable Pension Systems in the 21st Century.* Washington, DC: World Bank.

Weaver, R: Kent. (1998): The Politics of Pensions: Lessons from Abroad. In: Peter A. Diamond, A. Douglas Arnold, Michael J. Graetz and Alicia H. Munnell (eds), *Framing the Social Security Debate: Values, Politics and Economics.* Washington, DC: Brookings Institution Press for the National Academy of Social Insurance.

Whitehouse, E. (2000): Paying for Pensions: An International Comparison of Administrative Charges in Funded Retirement-Income Systems. Social Protection Paper Series, Discussion Paper No. 0021, Washington, DC, World Bank.

World Bank (1994): *Averting the Old Age Crisis: Policies to Protect the Old and Promote Growth.* New York: Oxford University Press.

NOTES

[1] The commune and kibbutz experiments provide no strong counter-arguments against the validity of this reasoning.

[2] Naturally, in place of the communities based on immediate (primary or original) relations, which one joins by virtue of being born (as described above), there is a steady development of new, modern systems of communities that a person elects to become a member of, and these do not usually have any economic or security functions – they are mostly "just for fun".

[3] Not without reason, it is ifrequently said of the poor, that having many children can be thought of as a sort of insurance. This phenomenon (alongside an improving healthcare system) goes a long way to explaining a large part of the demographic boom in developing countries.

[4] We will mostly leave the employer-organized (occupational) pension systems out of our future discussions. The reason for this is that their significance in Hungary is small (limited to payments to voluntary funds) and the expansion of their role is not currently on the agenda. And nor we will suggest any such thing here. Remark (2007): a recent appearance on the agenda has been made through implementation of the EU directive on occupational pension schemes, but we do not think this will significantly change the recent situation.

[5] (http://www.whitehouse.gov/omb/budget/fy2005/pdf/hist.pdf)

[6] AMECO is the annual macro-economic database of the European Commission's Directorate General for Economic and Financial Affairs (DG ECFIN).

[7] Those interested in the connections governing the planning of the individual's life cycle can find further details in the pamphlet by József Banyár: *Financial Planning of the Life Cycle (Az életpálya pénzügyi tervezése)*, Budapest, 2001.

[8] The figures based on the calculation for the necessery contribution level for cross-sectional equilibrium

[9] Espig-Andersen, *Averting the OldAge Crisis*, etc.

[10] Henceforth, basic concepts of pension insurance are introduced along the lines presented in the book *Averting the Old Age Crisis* (published by the World Bank in 1994).

[11] In what follows we will simply call this a "fund account system".

[12] For Pillar II.

[13] 1962

[14] 1968

[15] 35–64

[16] 50+

[17] 1989

[18] This was often the result even if the long-term balance of the system was also considered important when the system was introduced.

[19] Since the defined benefit is not strictly tied to savings, it follows that this promise will mean some insured receiving less than the level of benefits that is justified by their contributions, and others receiving more. And this will have the consequence of redistributing money from one insured to another.

[20] The contradiction between the defined benefit and the defined contribution systems is, in many ways, only formal. The calculation is the same in both systems, and only the variable parameters are different: in the defined benefit system it is the contribution, and in the defined contribution system it is the annuity – or at least it appears so at first sight. In reality, both the contribution and the annuity are variable parameters in both systems, because both have a desirable and an untenable level, and decision makers must maintain a balance between these. The difference lies only in the starting point of the iteration and where the final burden rests. In the case of the defined benefit system, the final burden is very often borne by a different generation, while in defined contribution systems there is a strong effort to keep the burden within the generation.

[21] Thus formally using the synonym for correctness!

[22] In the case of purely state bond investments, it is simply a matter of transforming the implicit state debt into an explicit one, so in several respects it is only a formal solution. At the same time, due to demographic changes, behind this there is a different kind of spreading of charging pension burdens, as in case of the pay-as-you-go system in the narrow sense.

[23] It should be mentioned that, due to the special social-economic situation, this happened differently in Hungary, and funding of the pension system did not appear on the radar screen. On the other hand – since almost all the tools of production were in the hands of the state – in a sense the Hungarian pension system before 1989 may be regarded as a special kind of funded system, because the vast state property stood behind the pension promises – only it was not directly assigned to the pension system. But a major part of this had been accumulated from the unpaid labour of earlier generations, so it would have been justified to regard it (also) as pension capital. This did not happen. During the process of privatization no thought was given to the funding of the pay-as-you-go pension system, and this is also seriously unfair.

[24] Incidentally, this is a feature of general thinking, and not especially of the left; but here we only examine those arguments that relate to the pay-as-you-go system, which is why the analysis has been narrowed down to this type of attitude.

[25] An in-built unfairness of pay-as-you-go systems – at least in Hungary, where slovenliness is in evidence in other areas, too – is the lack of precise registration. The system will consequently indeed be cheaper, but that should be no cause for celebration, since honest contribution payers are prevented from keeping "free-riders" out of the system. So the system is unfair to honest contribution payers and to those who can easily be targeted by the contribution collection authorities, and is rife with free-riders. The supporters of the system are denied the fairness they crave, and are forced to be solidaristic with those disrupting the system.

[26] As we saw above, this argument is much more justified in Hungary than in the West, since, for decades, the state accumulated working capital instead of the population, thanks to the latter's unpaid labour, and this property can be regarded as the implicit capital covering the implicit state debt behind the Hungarian pay-as-you-go system. Or rather it could have been while it existed. Incidentally, the state property that exists today could be credited – explicitly – totally to the state pension system. Making it explicit could help avoid the possibility that pensioners are left out of privatization, as happened in the 1990s – so we come back again to funding of the pay-as-you-go system.

[27] The development of the Hungarian pay-as-you-go system is rather unique. The country can be thought of as having "fallen into" the pay-as-you-go system, but in fact, in the system that existed between 1949 and 1989, thanks to state ownership, the pay-as-you-go system was virtually indistinguishable from a funded system. But there has been no formal assignation of (a large part of) state property to the pension system (assuming it was justified!), and so we can regard the pay-as-you-go system after 1989 as one created by a missed funding opportunity. Because of this, it is not necessarily true to say that the current pensioner population in Hungary has not paid back its generational debt, but this does not alter the fact, that there is a debt stock behind the pay-as-you-go system, and that we are rolling it forward.

[28] Naturally, rolling forward the debt stock may be economically rational if the interest on the debt is smaller than the investment yield of the capital behind the debt. But for this, the capital has to be in the hands of the debtor, which is not the case with implicit state debt.

[29] An exception is, for example, the fund account system that we propose to introduce, which could also be regarded as a pay-as-you-go system.

[30] It is surprising that, even though it is a plausible solution, the first such systems were introduced only at the end of the 1990s. Naturally, the accounting of entitlements existed earlier, though in a less comprehensive and less clear way (see the French pension system and the German earning-points system). The German earning points system can be regarded as a special version of the fund account system, even if the German earning points system is defined benefit, while a fund account system is defined contribution.

[31] Unless the loan was used to purchase property that is part of the legacy. We've seen that this is not the case with state debt, which usually finances consumption. This is certainly true of the state debt behind the pension system. Investments in infrastructure should be financed, primarily, from sources other than contribution payments. And state investments in working capital should be avoided.

[32] When the number of pensioners starts to decrease, then net repayment could also be on the agenda.

[33] Meaning its own state bonds!

[34] With the proviso that the defined benefit characteristic can remain in the case, for example, of pension annuities that have already started.

[35] The theoretical basis for this is that, without this tax, such citizens do not return to society the costs of their own upbringing.

[36] In reality, it is also unfair if the mortality changes of a given age group do not appear in the annuities already started. However, we do not put the

theoretical handling of this problem on the agenda now, because of the relatively low level of pension!

[37] Naturally, this requires a redistribution of contribution payments between genders in the entitlement accumulation phase! On the subject of the other parameters – e.g. bad habits and health status – it is only fair if the effects of these are taken account of in the healthcare system. While smoking decreases life expectancy and consequently raises the possible level of annuity (or decreases the volume of contribution payments necessary to achieve the same level of annuity!) it worsens the health status of the individual and in this way increases the expected health expenditure on that particular individual. So this factor has opposite financial effects in the two social security systems. Remark (2007): Although we still consider the differentiation of annuities according to gender to be right and fair, it no longer seems realistic, as it is forbidden under an EU directive. We consider this prohibition to be not proper and professionally problematic, but we nevertheless have to take it into consideration. The text has remained basically unchanged, but occasionally we remark that this is now no longer on the agenda.

[38] Naturally, we can see that, for economic policy considerations, the state temporarily pays from taxes the contribution of certain individuals. But this has to stay temporary and marginal.

[39] We should remark that, in theory, the shift could also be in the other direction, making a shift from Pillar II to Pillar I relatively simple. Politicians have already mooted this direction of shift, but in our view it would not be right or beneficial.

[40] It is very difficult to do this calculation subsequently, unless the fund value of the pension account – as with investment funds – is recorded in units. In this case, the task is easily solved. This is why we propose keeping records in units, even after commencement of an annuity.

[41] This transfer between accounts could be continuous throughout the marriage, but that would be more complicated and would give the same result as the method of transfer described here for "determinative events".

[42] Remark (2007): Now we are less certain about allowing unlimited top-up payments. The problem is that there is probably a correlation between the size of pension capital and the expected life span of the annuitant, so the possibility of making top-up payments can induce a strong adverse selection among annuitants. To counter this adverse selection, we can use one of two methods (or a combination of both): 1. setting an upper limit for an annuity from a private pension fund (over this limit it would be possible to withdraw the capital in a lump sum; it would be possible to supplement the capital only up to this limit); or 2. having the capital tranferred into an annuity using a degressive scale.

[43] Assuming that the annuities received from the two pillars always move together – starting, ending and being suspended at the same time; in practice, Pillar II will remain much more flexible than Pillar I for some time to come.

[44] The feature of pay-as-you-go systems – and thus also of the Hungarian system – that there is absolutely no intrinsic connection between the contribution payments made by the individual and the benefits received by him is typical of defined benefit systems in general – not just the pay-as-you-go system!

[45] Of course, it has to be acknowledged that this capital is "softer" than if it were formally printed/accounted as state debt.

[46] Naturally, for the fund account to be "real", the state must formally provide a guarantee that the sum of the account will be repaid (even if this guarantee stipulates that this will only be after retirement and only in the form of an annuity). With this guarantee, the balance of the fund account becomes real state debt; without this guarantee the system must not be started!

[47] Not only is the fund account system clearly not a pure pay-as-you-go type, but in fact it is only a small step from being a "classic", albeit somewhat specific, funded system. This small step is: the state debt recorded on the account has to be formally printed out as state debt.

[48] A wage tax, because we want to reserve the term "contribution" for money that is credited to the account; incidentally, the two are virtually the same, unless we differentiate between those making the payment – e.g. a contribution is paid by the individual and a wage tax by the employer. But the basis of this additional tax does not necessarily have to be the wage.

[49] Which means that we suppose the registry of the accounts even in the annuity phase, rather than just until the fund value is changed to annuity. Naturally, from this point on, the account will have a somewhat different character: it will be similar to the registry of the premium reserve of individual annuity insurance. On the one hand, this premium reserve constantly decreases by the annuity payments, and on the other hand it increases by the portion of the premium reserve of the deceased members of the risk community distributed among the individual members. Altogether, if mortality is close enough to the rate supposed at the time the annuity was calculated, then the balance of all accounts together is decreased by the benefit payments, even though the individual accounts of the annuitants still living decrease less – at the expense of the deceased annuitants, whose accounts drop to zero. Of course, mortality is never the same as supposed in the calculation. The difference is the profit or loss of the provider (in the fund account system at first this has to be the state!) – or this profit/loss can also be divided up among the members of the risk community (the annuitants)!

[50] Since implicit state debt can be created through other liabilities of the state; it is possible that, after the switch to the fund account system – temporarily – some parts of the former Pillar I still remain according to the former logic!

[51] At the same time, while there is a difference between implicit and explicit state debt for the state (because it handles one differently from the other – inappropriately, but possibly for good reason), investment in explicit state debt can also be taken into account.

[52] If the state "labels" its debt created this way, and assigns it unambiguously to the fund account system, then this can be regarded as making a part of the implicit state debt explicit, with no essential transactions being made. Of course, in this case the value of the implicit state debt has to be decreased by this "labelled" sum.

[53] Naturally, the state can perform the payment of its debts from the temporarily positive assets of the Monetary Fund, but this can be viewed as the state changing its explicit debt to implicit.

[54] Theoretically, this option can only be offered if the annuity benefits are calculated using the principle of individual equivalence – in other words, if the unisex mortality table (at least) has been scrapped. Until then, the risk of antiselection is too big. Remark (2007): Consequently, in practice it probably cannot be used for some time.

[55] We do not believe it is a "possibility" to ignore this issue, and simply to terminate the account, along with its balance value. This, by the way, would obliquely mean that the state would use these balance values to neutralize demographic fluctuations (in the bad years), or would simply swallow them (in the good years).

[56] Since we suggest removing the official retirement age, this age limit must be separately defined. Defining this limit can, in a sense, be "arbitrary", since it is already arbitrary that the disability subsystem does not provide benefits up to the death of the disabled person. The only reason for this is that we leave open the possibility of rehabilitating the disabled; we hope this will become rather more frequent an occurrence than it is at present. Thus the age limit can be set as the "normal" retirement age – e.g. we can put it at age 62 for a relatively long period of time.

[57] With the difference that, in the case of disabled persons, a special table that assumes a shorter remaining life expectancy is used when the starting annuity level is calculated. This means that, for the same amount of capital, they receive a higher pension, since the principle of actuarial correctness requires this.

[58] If we made the content of the account inheritable, then of course inheritance would also be a one-off account movement.

[59] If the owner of an account with a greater value dies, then the members of the risk community receive a greater legacy after him, so he also ought to receive a greater sum than the others!

[60] Remark (2007): To this question in 2003 we gave the answer "no", because we imagined an actuarially fair annuity. Since then it has transpired that there would probably be practical barriers of differentiation. Because of this, and also because the high annuity also causes adverse selection risk, we have changed our answer here.

[61] Naturally, this can be further refined; but we did not want to deal with this at present. It can also be changed to net substitution rate. The necessary level of contribution also naturally depends on which solution we choose in handling the accounts of those who die in the active phase of life.

[62] More precisely, as we shall see, the "small gross" wage!

[63] E.g. the substitution ratio is 50, because the usual 60% refers to the net wage.

[64] Remark (2007): At present a change to the law is in preparation.

[65] E.g. at present it is possible for the employer to make voluntary payments into Pillar II above the compulsory contribution. In the event of disability the compulsory and the voluntary payments are both transferred to Pillar I, but no excess benefits are provided for the excess payments.

[66] In reality, it is hard to find a theoretical base for setting the indexation level. Since the system supposes (implicit) state debt as covering pension annuities, it is a logical consequence that the interest on the accounts should be the usual interest on the state debt. But the problem with this is that the

yield of the state debt depends on the mass of the debt, and since the implicit state debt is not present on the market, it is not justified to assume the interest rate of the state debt open to the market as its yield. There are a number of arguments against using the gross wage index for setting the indexation level. The reason we felt its use to be justified in our proposal is that the income of the fund account system in a steady state grows precisely in accordance with the wage index (although we should remark that the fund account systems introduced so far have all abandoned this practice).

[67] We regard common-law marriage relationships, supported by a contract, in the same way as marriage.

[68] What we must ponder is that, even in the worst case (e.g. if the spouse divorces and takes part of the pension capital with him/her), the remaining pension capital should be sufficient to provide at least the social minimum as annuity, bearing in mind the current age of the insured.

[69] Since the income of the active spouse can be expected to be higher than the pension received later, this should not cause the family budget any problem!

[70] The correction should not be allowed to have a very great effect; all the same, it is useful for us to have a formal state guarantee that the correction will not make the nominal value of pensions decrease. But whatever else it does, the state must avoid exact projections and the risk that these guarantees will be "called upon".

[71] This is in a sharp distinction to the pension system, which, as we explained earlier, it is not expedient – even theoretically – to organize on a pay-as-you-go basis!

[72] Remark (2007): It seems that this year this will happen.

[73] Hint: What is the proportion of Hungarian citizens moving to Romania? And vice versa? This may be clear to a Hungarian reader, but not to an American.

[74] Or pay this part of the reserve in cash!

BOOKS PUBLISHED BY THE CENTER FOR HUNGARIAN STUDIES AND PUBLICATIONS

CHSP Hungarian Authors Series:
No. 1. *False Tsars.* Gyula Szvák. 2000.
No. 2. *Book of the Sun.* Marcell Jankovics. 2001.
No. 3. *The Dismantling of Historic Hungary: The Peace Treaty of Trianon,* 1920. Ignác Romsics. 2002.
No. 4. *The Soviet and Hungarian Holocausts: A Comparative Essay.* Tamás Krausz. 2006.

CHSP Hungarian Studies Series:
No. 1. *Emperor Francis Joseph, King of the Hungarians.* András Gero. 2001.
No. 2. *Global Monetary Regime and National Central Banking. The Case of Hungary, 1921–1929.* György Péteri. 2002.
No. 3. *Hungarian-Italian Relations in the Shadow of Hitler's Germany,* 1933–1940. György Réti. 2003.
No. 4. *The War Crimes Trial of Hungarian Prime Minister László Bárdossy.* Pál Pritz. 2004.
No. 5. *Identity and the Urban Experience: Fin-de-Siècle Budapest.* Gábor Gyáni. 2004.
No. 6. *Picturing Austria-Hungary. The British Perception of the Habsburg Monarchy,* 1865–1870. Tibor Frank. 2005.
No. 7. *Anarchism in Hungary: Theory, History, Legacies.* András Bozóki and Miklós Sükösd. 2006.
No. 8. *Myth and Remembrance. The Dissolution of the Habsburg Empire in the Memoir Literature of the Austro-Hungarian Political Elite.* Gergely Romsics. 2006.
No. 9. *Imagined History. Chapters from Nineteenth and Twentieth Century Hungarian Symbolic Politics.* András Gero. 2006.
No. 10. *Pál Teleki (1879–1941). A Biography.* Balázs Ablonczy. 2006.
No. 11. *The Hungarian Revolution of 1956. Myths and Realities.* László Eörsi. 2006.

No. 12. *The Jewish Criterion in Hungary.* András Gero. 2007.

No. 13. *Remember Hungary 1956. Essays on the Hungarian Revolution and War of Independence in American Memory.* Tibor Glant. 2007.

No. 14. *Reflections on Twentieth Century Hungary: A Hungarian Magnate's View.* Baron Móric Kornfeld. 2007.

No. 15. *Ideas on Territorial Revision in Hungary 1920–1945.* Miklós Zeidler. 2007.

No. 16. *Hungarian Illusionism.* András Gero. 2008.

No. 17. *Romanians in Historic Hungary.* Ambrus Miskolczy. 2008.

No. 18. *The Kingdom of Hungary and the Habsburg Monarchy in the Sixteenth Century.* Géza Pálffy. 2008.

No. 19. *A Possible and Desirable Pension System.* József Banyár and József Mészáros. 2009.

Nyomdai munkák:
mondAt Kft. • Budapest
www.mondat.hu